Underground
MANCHESTER

Underground
MANCHESTER

KEITH WARRENDER

Willow
PUBLISHING

Willow Publishing
36 Moss Lane
Timperley
Altrincham
Cheshire WA15 6SZ

ISBN 978-0-946361-41-0

Book designed by Keith Warrender

Printed by EWS Colour Print
Buckley, Flintshire

Photo title page: Ardwick tunnel by Les Patterson

Dedicated to the memory of Harry Smith,
a tireless explorer of underground Manchester

Contents

Warning

Foreword

By KEN HOWARTH

My first encounter with Manchester's subterranean history was in the late 1960s whilst working for the Co-operative Wholesale Society in Manchester. It was my first job, and I was given the responsibility along with lots of other youngsters working in the Postal Department, of delivering the morning mail. This meant going round to different departments in the Balloon Street area dropping off the morning post. Manchester in the 1960s was often wet and on one particular day I went off to deliver the usual post when the young man I was with took one look outside and told me to follow him - which I did. He took me down into various basements and passageways linking buildings in the Balloon Street complex eventually emerging somewhere near Garden Street, next to Dantzig Street near Shude Hill. The system as I recall was planned to make delivery and access to the different departments easier, it certainly made my job easier and drier!

Then in the early 1970s, a fledgling BBC Radio Manchester, in conjunction with the Workers' Educational Association commissioned me to explore Manchester's history for a series of radio programmes. Local radio was still experimental and out-of-the-studio reportage on local history virtually unknown, so when the BBC's Chris Walmsley and the WEA's Wally Long agreed on this pioneering approach, I was only too happy to assist. The series was to consist of a mix of on-site reportage and oral history. We visited coal mines, travelled on canals and even rode on the footplate of a steam locomotive, but by far the most interesting of all the series was Manchester Underground.

The BBC still had the power in its name to open doors almost without question. Granada TV allowed us to explore the tunnel of the Manchester and Salford Junction Canal, and with British Rail to explore the newly discovered tunnel beneath the fish dock at Manchester Victoria Station. This 'open sesame' also allowed us to explore the hidden world below the Victoria Street arches and the catacombs under Central Station.

I doubt that today the raft of Health and Safety legislation and attendant paranoia would allow us to do many of the things we achieved in the 1970s. Yes, I was lowered down a well on a bucket, and yes, I did paddle along the water-filled tunnel of the Manchester and Salford Junction Canal, and slithered down enormous piles of rubbish beneath Central Station to find the locks. We explored the secret world of the Ardwick tunnels (notorious for accumulations of noxious gases).

These were calculated risks; what the listener did not know was that we had the expertise of Manchester City Council's engineers behind us, as well as a Coal Mines Rescue expert, expert canoeists, industrial archaeologists, divers, and structural engineers. These wonderful people were not paid by the BBC, they were as keen as we were to explore that unknown world beneath the city and all volunteered their services. Exciting times indeed.

After reading a booklet we produced for the series, Keith Warrender approached me and asked if I would be willing to co-operate in this new book on Manchester's world beneath our feet; I was only too pleased to help in any way I could.

Although much of my professional life has been in museums and archives (I was founder and Director of North West Sound Archive), I have maintained a parallel professional level of interest in geology throughout my adult life. To understand Manchester's hollow world, it is necessary to understand a little about the nature of its geology in the simplest terms. It is incidentally a story of climate change.

Ken (right) preparing to broadcast

When Manchester was a sub-tropical forest

Imagine a jam sandwich cake. The bottom part of the cake consists of rocks formed 350 million years ago during the Carboniferous period when Manchester was part of a long-lost environment. Huge trees 50-100 feet high grew in a dense forest of an almost unimaginable size. Truly they were not trees as we know them today but giant horsetails. The climate was oxygen-rich and warm. Gradually these trees fell and decayed, forming over the millennia, coal. The marshy areas of the forest were frequently inundated by river deposits such as sand, now surviving as sandstone, often above the coal. Deeper conditions produced muds which became shales. This process of sed-

9

imentary deposition continued in cycles for millions of years resulting in numerous coal seams around Manchester and elsewhere.

So what was in the middle layer of our cake? Climate change occurred yet again. At the end of the Carboniferous period conditions changed and the rocks tell of a warm marine environment with lime-rich rocks largely made up of the microscopic organic remains of aquatic animals including fish. These rocks known as the Ardwick lime-stones were extensively worked from underground caverns in the area. Access to these workings is no longer possible, although the caverns explored by the BBC in the 1970s are now thought to be part of this almost unknown extensive mining and quarrying activity on the boundaries of the city centre.

When Manchester was an arid desert

Then there is a problem, for someone has removed a layer from our cake. Nature herself over millions of years eroded away many thousands of feet of rock, creating what geologists call an unconformity. On that ancient Carboniferous surface a new rock was deposited dating from an age of deserts and arid conditions - the Permo-Triassic period of some 225-280 million years ago. The remains of these

Fire-clay working at Ardwick

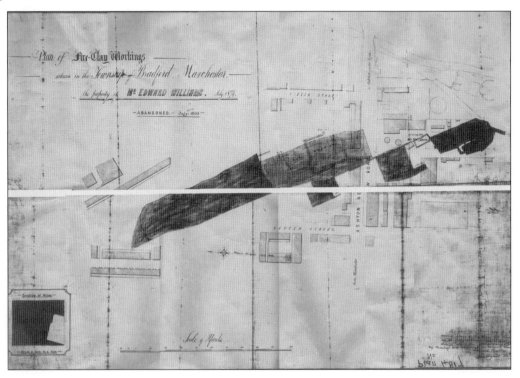

ancient deserts still lie beneath the City, including their fossilised sand dunes being clearly visible where the rocks are exposed at the surface. The first in this sequence is the Collyhurst sandstone with 'millet seed' structure characteristic of wind-driven desert sands. The Manchester Marls, a limestone often made of broken shell fragments some 200 feet in thickness come next. Gradually the rocks become sandy in nature giving way to the Sherwood sandstone, which outcrops on the banks of the Irwell and underlies much of the city centre. This sandstone, as the name implies, is best exposed in Nottinghamshire, and is a soft red sandstone formed by water in arid conditions in a series of huge braided deltas during seasonal storms.

Both the Carboniferous coal measures rocks and the later Permo-Triassic rocks were subsequently tilted by earth movements to about 1 in 3 and 1 in 7 (steep stairs at home) to the south-west. This accounts for the outcropping of coal seams to the east of the city towards Bradford and their occurrence at depth to the west. The sandstones and marls from above the coal measures are easy to work and many of the subterranean excavations in Manchester are in these rocks.

'Iceberg' boulder in Manchester University quadrangle

Enter the Ice Age

Now for the ice on our cake. There was one more geological event in our story - the Great Ice Age. Around 1.6 million years ago the climate became intensely cold and a series of glaciations took place, the main one forming a vast ice sheet covering much of the Northern Hemisphere including Scotland, England, Ireland and Wales. Under the thick ice sheet a layer of ground-up material was formed known as boulder clay - till to the modern geologist. The deposit varies in thickness according to the lie of the land on which it was created. In the city centre it is relatively thin - hence the excavations in the underlying rocks described earlier.

An iceberg in Manchester

Although fairly easy to excavate, boulder clay was not without problems. In 1888 when sewers were being excavated under Oxford Street, a large boulder was encountered. The boulder was found to be a glacial erratic. This was far from being a small boulder, being 9 ft 6 inches by 7 ft 4 inches. Modern thinking suggests it was probably brought down from the Lake District trapped in an iceberg during a warm phase; the ice melted, leaving the erratic beneath Oxford Street to vex the Victorian tunnellers. The rock is now preserved in the main quadrangle at the University of Manchester.

STORRIE DENTIST

CIGARS.

A.KUIT.

IRONMONGERS.CUTLE[RY]

MATS   BRUSHES

TEA URNS   DISH COVERS   [A]SH PANS

FENDERS   [FI]RE [IRONS]

FURNISHING CUTLERY &

CROMWELL

Introduction

When I set out to discover what lay below the city streets and landmarks, I found mention of a lost city, an unused tube station, mysterious rail systems, old streets and shops, and secret passages. Do these stories hold any truth? Of course there is no dispute about the presence of sewers and all the service workings, which have been described as just as impressive as the buildings above. But this book is mainly about other underground routes, tunnels and spaces. Are they simply 'urban myths' or is there proof of their existence?

Perhaps wiser writers have looked at this subject and decided there were too many difficulties to proceed further. Sometimes the information is sparse, and lots of potential evidence has been crushed by building redevelopment. This letter highlights the problems of the tunnel researcher.

> '*My father-in-law works for Manchester Corporation Highways and Sewers Department in the Bury New Road district. On numerous occasions they have come across tunnels when digging a sewer, or the ground or road has subsided in the district where your tunnels are. The Corporation men just fill in the hole or the tunnels because it would have meant a lot of trouble to them if they reported it, with archaeologists and historians investigating and holding their work up. So over the years these tunnels will have been filled in.*'
> D CAWTHORNE 1973 (JH)*

Even during 2007, while working on this publication I got to know of a local historian encountering great difficulties in gaining access to a significant underground site before it disappeared for ever under a new development. So there is the heart of the problem. Any tunnels uncovered during building or maintenance work are generally not going to be examined by experts. There is the old saying 'time is money', and for councils and companies there can be no delay in the

Here's a discovery that was recorded - an old wooden drain

JOY HANCOX ARCHIVE

An underground space still exists beneath the site of the Cromwell statue which used to stand on Victoria Street, at the corner of Cateaton Street. The statue is now in Wythenshawe Park

work schedule. Work cannot be suspended and minutes, then hours tick away while someone is sent for to make notes, take measurements and photographs. The only exception to this is when human bones or coffins are unearthed and then there has to be a pause while the remains are either examined on site or removed.

So the contractor's bulldozer can be both an obstacle to our knowledge, but also our excuse if the evidence has been destroyed. However, despite all the problems, there is clearly much fascination in these matters - a growing number of web sites cover it, with varying degrees of accuracy and speculation. I've thought for some time that this was an area of historical interest waiting to be tackled and so here, for the first time, is a collection of accounts from many different sources, of tunnels, passages and other underground spaces around Manchester.

Some readers will be aware of Ken Howarth's excellent pamphlet which linked with his local radio series exploring under the city in

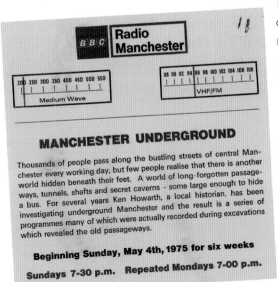

BBC Radio Manchester

200 250 300 350 400 450 500 550
Medium Wave

88 90 92 94 96 98 100 102 104 106 108
VHF/FM

MANCHESTER UNDERGROUND

Thousands of people pass along the bustling streets of central Manchester every working day, but few people realise that there is another world hidden beneath their feet. A world of long-forgotten passageways, tunnels, shafts and secret caverns - some large enough to hide a bus. For several years Ken Howarth, a local historian, has been investigating underground Manchester and the result is a series of programmes many of which were actually recorded during excavations which revealed the old passageways.

Beginning Sunday, May 4th, 1975 for six weeks

Sundays 7-30 p.m.   Repeated Mondays 7-00 p.m.

1975. The material was an inspiration for me, and set me on the underground trail. A few years ago I put some of my findings into an illustrated talk to present to local groups. I have found it a popular subject and people often comment that they knew nothing of these underground routes, even though they have lived or worked around Manchester for many years. I always look forward to the questions session after the talk because, invariably, people give me other snippets of information. Also, questions are asked which either give more clues or send me back to make further investigations.

I have only been able to proceed with the book because of the work done by others. I have already mentioned Ken Howarth, but should also include Joy Hancox and Harry Smith and family. Without their generous help and advice this publication might never have happened. There is more about their contribution and their own work later on.

During the course of my research I've come across many amazing stories about underground Manchester. By bringing these widespread accounts together, we begin to have a more accurate impression of tunnel routes in and around the City. As I've mapped them out, a wide network of routes emerges which deserves more thorough investigation. We may not always come to firm conclusions about the origins or purpose of some of the tunnels because of the difficulties previously described. Often it is a case of presenting the known information and allowing the reader to decide.

Wherever possible, I have used first hand accounts of entering tunnels, but in other instances we have to rely on the experiences of the friends and acquaintances of writers. Often several people writing independently talk of the same place which adds weight to the story. The reports are from people in all walks of life - the business community, council workers, journalists, residents with memories from childhood, and office and shop workers. Sometimes it is frustrating that people will say they knew of a tunnel but did not go along it. We wonder why they didn't explore it and find out exactly where it led. The answer is often, quite reasonably, fear for their own safety - old tunnels are dangerous places. There would be the possibility of roof collapse, poisonous gases, getting lost, and of course rats. So it was safer and more sensible just to know the whereabouts of a tunnel rather than enter it. Many of the better-known engineering or commercial tunnels are well doc-

Harry Smith (left) and Steve Coyle excavating the Castlefield tunnel

umented, but so many other routes and underground spaces were built in seeming secrecy and without record, and yet well known in the locality.

The book is also about what have might been, eg the Picc-Vic Tunnel and the efforts to bring an underground railway network to the city. Also included are details of many old industrial workings, now covered over by later developments.

One thing is certain, this book could not have been written without the contributions of the many people who have willingly written in response to newspaper articles or TV programmes. They put their names and addresses to their recollections so they must have been personally convinced of the story. The letters were written in the 1970s mainly by older people remembering things from their childhood, or what others had told them. Some share their business or work experiences. Because this was around thirty years ago, many of them will now have died, so we are glad that they shared information that is simply not available elsewhere.

I will attempt to explain some of the mysteries about underground Manchester, but in the best traditions of the subject, it will still leave much for the reader to advance their own ideas. I'm sure this book will not satisfy everyone. 'Conspiracy theorists' may think the book doesn't go far enough, although I have tried my best to uncover the facts. Sometimes institutions and organisations keep the truth very deeply buried, or are simply unwilling to pass on the most basic information. For those who believe a tunnel network under Manchester is just a myth, the experiences recounted here will give cause for reconsideration. Others may find here confirmation of stories they have already heard but have never quite known whether to believe them.

There may be some who will think that the existence of tunnels, other than the well-publicized projects are just not possible. I would draw your attention to a speech given by Dr WB Wright to the Manchester Literary and Philosophical Society in 1939 in which he outlined the possibilities of such a system. He had just completed a fifteen year geological survey of Lancashire and thought the red sandstone could provide solutions for traffic congestion as well as a wartime refuge during air raids. 'The thing to do would be to dig down somewhere near Exchange Station, and once in the sandstone it would be possible to drive tunnels in various directions.' He admitted there would be problems with water, as the constructors of the Guardian bunker were to find out, but he said that was a problem for engineers. He thought it quite possible to bore routes to Bolton, St Helens and to almost any distance in the south. If the tunnels were to be used as war-time shelters they would need to be between 50 and 100 feet below ground. Dr Wright's ideas may have been merely academic theories but, unbeknown to him, there is evidence to suggest that there was a tunnel network with a hub very close to Exchange Station already in existence.

Manchester Corporation had already realised the possibilities and had published proposals a few months previously to construct north-south and east-west routes under the city centre. Roads would slope down into the red sandstone rock and would also be used as air-raid shelters. Mr FE Button, the Chief City Engineer, costed the project at £2 million and estimated it would take three years to complete. It was even planned to link in with an underground rail system.

In the 1970s when it seemed, at last, a certainty that Manchester was to have a high speed tube, the 19 test boreholes down to 90 feet

The Rochale Canal where it passes beneath Piccadilly and Dale Street

along the proposed route provided satisfactory results and led the consulting engineers to conclude that nothing had been revealed to cause them to change the route. Therefore in the opinion of geologists and civil engineers over the last seventy years, tunnelling under Manchester is a viable option and would help to ease many transportation problems.

Although I have tried to uncover as much as possible about the underground spaces around Manchester, readers may be able to confirm details or may know of other places. If you have any further information, or I have been inaccurate please contact me and I will consider it for future publication. It was not possible to cover adequately the huge amount of mining activity in the area, but there is a section on Bradford Colliery and references to others. You will also note that I have included information about what lies above the underground sites where it seems of particular relevance or interest.

I would remind readers that all the places mentioned in this book, unless advertised as visitor attractions, are strictly prohibited and not to be entered - see the warning on page seven. My main aim, through this book, is to reveal many surprising things which lie below the city. Here, for the first time are the collected accounts of many people who have seen it for themselves, which put together with information from other sources, will be a revelation to many.

Keith Warrender, October 2007

18

The Manchester and Salford Junction Canal Tunnel

In 1799 there had been proposals for a canal link from the River Irwell to the Rochdale Canal, but it was not until 1836 that a Bill was sent to Parliament. The link was proposed as a commercial venture because of the difficulties of off-loading goods at the river and transporting them along the congested City streets.

The Bill was passed, and at a cost of £60,000 the canal was built by the Mersey and Irwell Company to connect the Mersey and Irwell rivers with the Rochdale Canal. This was in response to the Bridgewater Canal Company's new canal link from the River Irwell into Castlefield in 1838 which charged high tolls. Another consideration was the Manchester Bolton and Bury Canal which joined with the Irwell from the coal mining districts of Bolton and Bury, which could also connect to the Rochdale Canal.

As the route of the Manchester and Salford Junction Canal went across the city, a short distance after entering the canal from the Irwell, by Water Street, a 499-yard tunnel had to be built between Charles Street and Watson Street. The wording of the Act is not conclusive, but the tunnel may have been excavated as a cutting and then roofed over. A gasometer by the western entrance of the tunnel supplied power for the lamps every thirty yards. The canal then entered locks on the site of the present Manchester Central (previously known as G-Mex), and from here it linked up with the Rochdale Canal near Great Bridgewater Street.

The canal opened to traffic - boats and barges - on 28 October 1839 but it was never a commercial success. Costing £57 per linear yard, it was an expensive project, not only with the cost of the tunnel, but also because of the installation of two pumps to maintain water levels, along with the construction of four locks to accommodate the rise of 40 feet from west to east along the route.

The old west entrance of the tunnel at Grape Street

Ken Howarth

Water had to be drawn only from from the River Irwell because the Rochdale Canal owners would not allow water to be used from their waterway. There were also early setbacks when one of the locks collapsed, followed by severe frosts which temporarily closed the canal. The pumping engines which had to draw water from the Irwell did not work well, and the shareholders were forced to put in more money to maintain the workings.

Although the canal had been an impressive engineering feat, with a tunnel, locks, storage reservoir, pump houses and byewater tunnels, the amount of traffic along the canal was disappointing. This was due to the Bridgewater Canal Company which had opened new locks at Hulme and immediately lowered the tolls on its route, which was also an easier waterway to navigate.

A second Act was passed in 1840 to raise £25,000 in shares, but this was not enough to save the ailing company and two years later the loss-making canal was offered to the Mersey and Irwell Navigation Company, which in 1845 was bought by the rival Bridgewater Canal Company. The canal's lack of success continued, and in the early 1870s the Manchester and Salford Junction Canal was receiving less than £1000 annually in tolls. The 'railway revolution', starting in the 1840s, made most canals unprofitable.

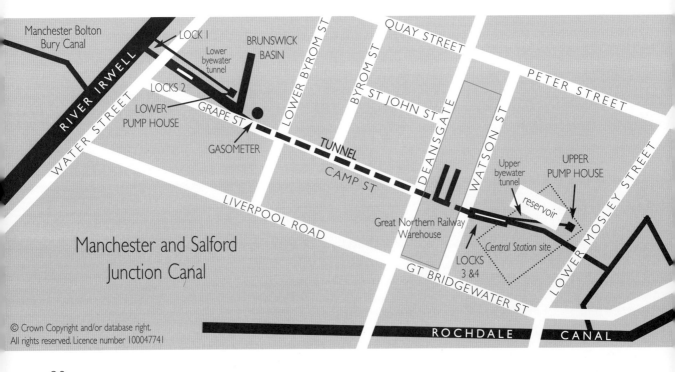

Manchester and Salford
Junction Canal

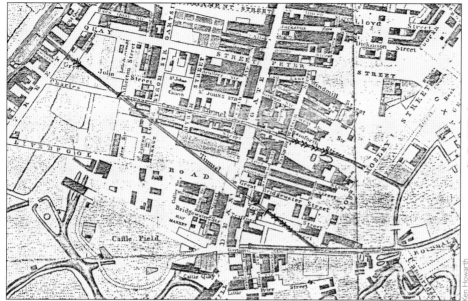

An 1813 map showing two projected paths for the canal. It is not known why the shorter route to join the Rochdale Canal at a lower level was not adopted.

Ken Howarth

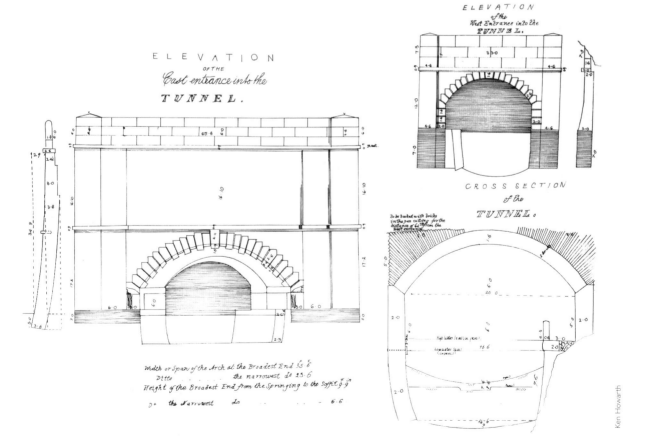

ELEVATION
OF THE
East entrance into the
TUNNEL.

ELEVATION
of the
West Entrance into the
TUNNEL.

CROSS SECTION
of the
TUNNEL.

Width or Span of the Arch at the Broadest End 35·6
Ditto   the narrowest   do. 25·6
Height of the Broadest End from the Springing to the Soffit 9·9

do. the Narrowest   do. . . . . 6·6

Ken Howarth

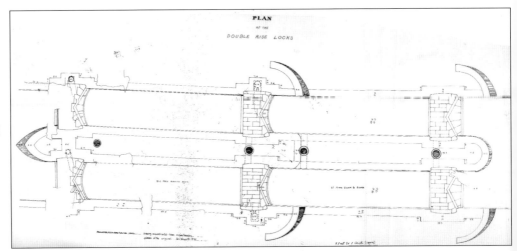

PLAN

of the

DOUBLE RISE LOCKS

Double rise locks 3
and 4 by the east
entrance to the tunnel

1938 inspection of the
trans-shipment dock

However, the location of the canal generated other commercial activity, with two slate wharves, boat and timber yards and a potato market at the western terminal. Also, four adjacent textile mills are thought to have drawn water from the canal.

The section of the canal between Watson Street and the Rochdale canal was closed in 1875 and backfilled. It became the site of Central Station in 1880 - the last main passenger railway terminus to be built in Manchester.

In a letter to the *Manchester City News* in 1882 the writer had come across the tunnel in his boyhood:

> '...I found on one of my rambles a canal tunnel with a towing-path for horses. I passed through and found that it came out near the Black Horse Hotel, Alport Town, where now stands the Central Station ...
> I have been speaking to an old waterman, who has gone with boats for Rochdale under this tunnel for years before the Central Station was thought of, and who tells me that the Central Station end is bricked up, and that the old tunnel is full of old boats or flats from one end to the other. The end near to Charles Street is boarded up.' [1]

Great Northern Railway Warehouse, Deansgate

The remaining part of the tunnel continued in commercial operation, and with the building of the adjoining Great Northern Railway Warehouse in 1898 it was more fully used. Two branch tunnels were built in 1900 off the main tunnel, possibly after an old disused canal arm had been discovered. From two lift shafts, goods were hoisted from a trans-ship ment dock to the six levels of the warehouse. This facility meant that goods could be taken from the warehouse through to the Ship Canal via the Manchester and Salford Junction Canal and the River Irwell. This continued until around 1922 when work ing ceased and the Canal was officially closed for commercial traffic in 1936.

The tunnel came into a different use during the Second World War when it was drained to become a shelter during the Manchester Blitz. In a report to Air Raid Precautions Special Committee in 1939, signed by the City Engineer, Surveyor, Architect and Chief Constable, detailed information is given about the structure. The tunnel was 1600 feet long, 20 feet wide and 17 feet high. Overhead cover varied along the route. The arch of the tunnel was 18 inches thick and mostly in good condition. The capacity was estimated at 5000 people, on the basis of the Home Office's rule of 6 sq feet per person. It was to be accessible to anyone within ten minutes walk of the tunnel. A bomb-proof dam was to be built across the entrance and a drain down to the river so that pumps would not be required. The ownership of the tunnel remained with the Manchester Ship Canal Company, who had listed it as an asset in 1904, but maintenance during the War years was transferred to Manchester Corporation.[2]

Plans to convert the Manchester and Salford Junction Canal into an air raid shelter

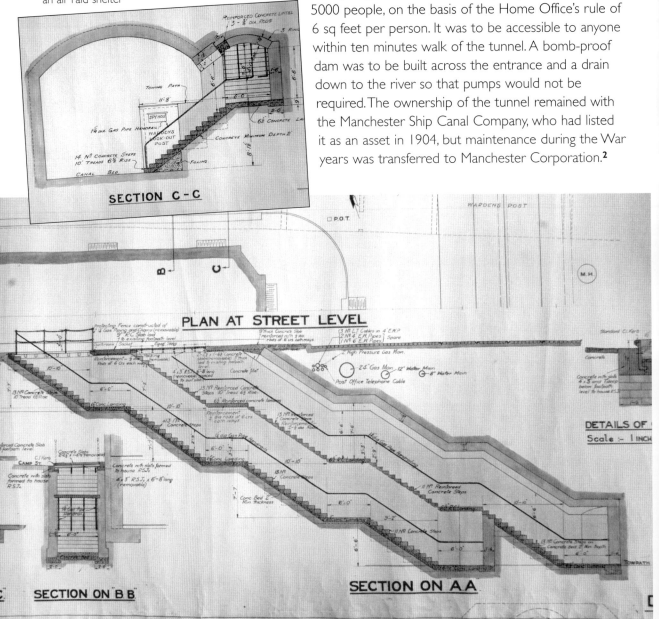

SECTION C-C

PLAN AT STREET LEVEL

SECTION ON 'B B'

SECTION ON A A

ARP Committee members inspecting the tunnel in 19

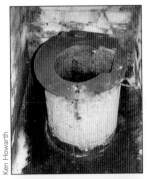

War-time relics found in the tunnel during the 1976 exploration

The Civil Defence Scheme arranged for sixteen blast-walls to be installed, approximately every 100 feet, to restrict bomb damage. An ARP warden's lookout post is still there today. The estimated cost of £18,000 to convert the tunnel also included handrails at the entrances, chemical toilets, water supply, lighting from the mains, an emergency diesel generator, electric fans and a filtered air system.

During the war, entrances to the tunnel were made in Grape Street, Lower Byrom Street, Byrom Street, Deansgate and Watson Street.

The use of the tunnel as an air-raid shelter officially finished on 11 May 1948, and the entrances were sealed. The original estimated capacity had been reduced to 1368 people.[3]

The ARP warden's lookout post

.Although most of the tunnel was used as public shelters, a section was reserved for woolspinners Copley-Smith and Sons of Lower Mosley Street. Their part of the shelter was 55 feet long and 20 feet wide. There was seating along the sides and the floor was covered as a protection against damp with a layer of cinders and with duckboards. The shelter had electric light, power plugs for radio, and an emergency store of food, as well as a small retiring compartment, in which 'anyone who might faint during a raid could recover quickly without causing distress or hysteria among the other occupants of the shelter.'

War time memories

One local person described the tunnel as *'the biggest and safest shelter in Manchester, but it was running with water and it was terrible! There were beds of all kinds - it was like a doss house! People from all round Manchester took their beds down there - you used to see them coming from Cheetham Hill with packs on their backs at night.'* [4]

A Manchester Evening News reader remembered the Camp Street shelter: *'It saved hundreds of lives. My family and hundreds of others would run the gauntlet from Hulme over the bridge to Deansgate every night before the bombs fell. We had beds and blankets for all our needs and we felt safe, and next morning we walked home and felt how lucky we were to be alive.*

I was the eldest of five children and will never forget the bombing of Manchester that horrendous Christmas. I recall climbing to the top of the stairs to find the whole of Deansgate on fire. It was unbelievable. The shelter was cold, black and damp, but it was a second home to us - a lifesaver'. [5]

Another resident remembered: *'We slept there most nights when the sirens went, until the all clear. There was a canteen down there selling tea ,coffee, Oxo and a few snacks because most people came in straight from work. Bunk beds were built along the damp walls, and people took their own bedding.'* [6]

One local has sad memories of the shelter, recalling the night of the 1940 Christmas Blitz. There was a huge bang which seemed very close, and the lights went out in the tunnel which made people panicky. When they got out in the morning, they found their homes in nearby Duke Street had all been blown up - everything they possessed had gone.[7] People remember the sound of chattering down there - mothers sharing the latest news. They would also take it in turns staying awake to look after the children.

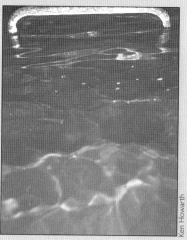

Ken Howarth

Ken Howarth

The tunnel had filled with water
by the time of the 1976 exploration.

After presenting two BBC local radio programmes about the tunnel
and then taking part in an official exploration in 1976, Ken Howarth
described what he saw:

'The tunnel is brick-lined throughout, although at the Deansgate end the soft
red permo-trias sandstone was exposed in the sides of the tunnel and chisel
marks were clearly visible. Another interesting feature of the tunnel was the
presence of numerous stalactites on the soffit in the side passages formed
since the last war by water percolating through the brickwork and dissolving
and re-depositing the lime contained in the mortar. In one part of the tunnel
there is evidence that the roof had collapsed and had to be rebuilt. In fact
immediately above the point of the collapse is Camp Street a road in everyday use.

The course of the tunnel passes close by the former St John's graveyard, and
tree roots had begun to penetrate through the brickwork in the tunnel arch.
The towpath was examined for traces of the gas lighting installed in 1839
and a number of heavily corroded iron brackets were found but could not be
accurately identified as gas fittings.

The tunnel has a distinct kink in its alignment, probably a surveying error.
At several places along the tunnel there are remains of air-raid shelter fitments
including iron bed frames, a warden's helmet, elsan toilets, various warning

The tunnel in 1994

notices, as well as the old entrance steps that once led down from the surface. Near Deansgate it is possible to walk on the raised bed of the canal, a dry course surface having been laid during ARP days. A short distance further along the tunnel it unexpectedly widens into a chamber of substantial dimensions. The chamber is now divided into two by a blastwall, but it was originally around 125 feet in length and 23 feet 6in in height.

Along the north side was a dock with two passageways leading to separate hoistwells giving access to the GNR warehouse above. One iron bollard for mooring the boats to the docks still survives and a short distance away it is possible to examine one of two passageways leading to the former hoists. The passage which is about 8 feet wide, led to an iron gate in front of the hoist shaft. Beyond the canal chamber the end of the tunnel is now reached. The ARP's merciless installation of access steps has revealed much of the original entrance arch to the tunnel, estimated at being 34 feet 6in in diameter. The top part of the tunnel entrance was revealed in a section beneath the Central Station complex.

The area of Central Station was built across the site of the upper locks and spanned the then disused section of the canal on a huge arch. The section was examined during a radio programme about canals in 1972. At that time the twin locks were no longer visible, having been backfilled. [8]

This is John C Fletcher's account of the tunnel in 1989.

> '... descending a ladder which brought me to the eight-feet -thick
> obstructing wall on the old Central Station boundary, I was able
> to walk through the massive portal of the original tunnel. I passed
> under the Great Northern Warehouse (where the old goods lift shafts
> still exist), through all the accoutrements of air raid shelters (including
> chemical toilets!), by the various staircases which had been the shelter
> entrances, under Deansgate, and continued for over a quarter of
> a mile to the basement of Granada'. [9]

Granada TV bought the western canal terminus area in 1955, but
within a year had put their section of the tunnel up for sale, stating
they had no use for it. They had originally planned to use the twelve
feet high tunnel for film processing and editing, but following the
purchase of nearby property had changed their plans. The tunnel still
remains under their ownership, although the old Brunswick Basin on
their site had been filled in with Blitz debris after the last war. When
the basin was in use there was a slate wharf, graving dock, stables
and workshops.

Restored lock by the River Irwell.

The only overground signs of the canal today are the restored locks
at the western end next to the Victoria and Albert Hotel, Water
Street, and the rebuilt eastern link to the Rochdale Canal, which
includes the former route under Bridgewater Street and the
Bridgewater Basin on the site of the old canal. There have been
proposals by Granada TV and the Great Northern to open the
tunnel as a visitor attraction but, to date, no further progress has
been made on these ventures, and entry remains restricted.

The ashlar blocks of the original towpath can
still be seen in the underpass to Bridgewater Hall.

The restored link to the Rochdale Canal,
beneath Great Bridgewater Street

The canal tunnel 1

31

The canal east of Mosley Street towards Central Station

Filled-in section of the canal beyond Mosley Street, during an inspection c1971

Ken Howarth

Ken Howarth

ELEVATION
of
GREAT BRIDGEWATER STREET BRIDGE

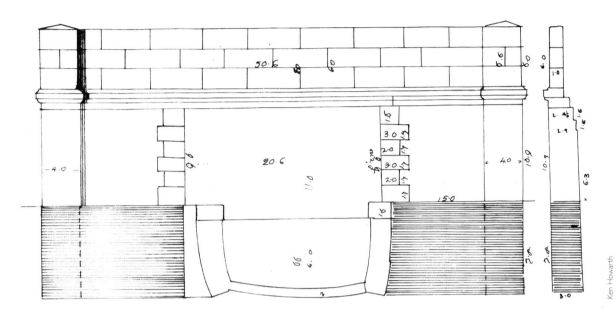

Ken Howarth

The tunnel is well lit with gas, these being placed at a distance of only twenty yards from each other. A towing path runs along the whole length of it, on which are stationed servants of the Company to assist where required in the hauling of vessels.

The canal is supplied with water from the river Irwell by two powerful engines being stationed on the banks of the canal (one about half way between Water Street and Atherton Street, and the other near the reservoir between Lower Mosley Street and Watson Street) to force up the water into it above the locks. The engines are of remarkable construction and each are capable of raising about seven hundred gallons of water at a stroke and working at about ten strokes a minute. Thus by means of these engines the whole of this capacious canal above the locks, supposing it to be empty, can be supplied with sufficient water in less than fifteen minutes.

The engines themselves are well worthy of attention being constructed on a new principle invented by Mr Andrew Knowles, (one of the directors of the company) the chief feature of which, that the cylinders are placed over the pits and the pumps directly over the piston rods. By this means a vast saving in machinery is effected as well as of brick and stonework with the construction of the enginehouses. Indeed the enginehouses of these powerful machines are no longer than an ordinary cottage, and the engines themselves occupy a space of only four yards by two. They have been erected by Messrs Walker Brothers of Bury.

From the MANCHESTER CHRONICLE AND SALFORD STANDARD 2 November 1839

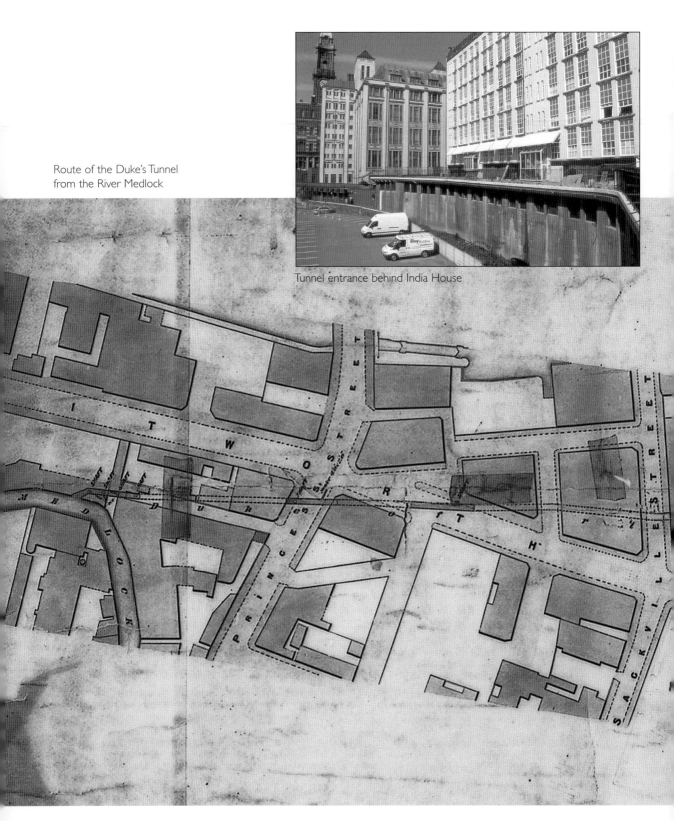

Route of the Duke's Tunnel
from the River Medlock

Tunnel entrance behind India House

34

The Duke's Tunnel

India House and Lancaster House, Whitworth Street

Whitworth Street is one of Manchester's finest streets with its towering warehouses, and offices. At the rear of India House, the remains of Manchester's industrial past are to be seen. Just visible from the car park backing onto the River Medlock is the top of an arch rising above the river.

This is the entrance to the Duke's Tunnel which runs from the River Medlock, under India House and Lancaster House on Whitworth Street. It then passes below the junction of Whitworth Street and Princess Street, Sackville Street, Chorlton Street and under Minshull Street, before ending beneath the Piccadilly Station approach.

Boats travelled up the River Medlock from Castlefield laden with coal from the Duke of Bridgewater's mines at Worsley and entered the tunnel close to Old Garratt dye works. The 'Worsley Yard Book' records its dimensions as 649 yards long, 8 feet 6 high by 6 feet wide. It took three years to build, starting in April1787, and on 21 April 1789 the *Manchester Mercury* reported that three vessels carrying coal by this route from the Duke of Bridgewater's mines had arrived at Bank Top for the first time.[1]

Silted up tunnel entrance

United Utilities

The tunnel was to have a short commercial life because, by around 1800, the river had silted up. The water level had risen by at least eight feet, making it impossible to use. The entrance is only partially visible today.

The line of the tunnel roughly follows Shooters Brook, which on Green's 1794 map of Manchester, remained a pleasant open field area. The Brook rises in Newton Heath and was originally known as Snipe's Brook, but it seems to have got its later name from the shooting of birds - particularly snipe - around the area where Piccadilly Station is situated.

The Duke's tunnel ended below the approach to Piccadilly Station, previously known as London Road

The canal entrance used to be separate from the exit for the brook. There are accounts of a weir near the entrance, where children would play and swim through an underwater opening to bring out coal from an old boat in the tunnel.[2]

The coal boats worked up and down the tunnel by 'legging'. The men lay on their backs and used their legs on the top or sides of the tunnel. At Shooters Brow, near the junction of London Road and Ducie Street, there was a shaft through which the coal was winched up by a horse-powered crane, known as a 'horse gin', at Knowles and Son's coal yard.[3]

However, the continual silting of the Medlock by mills and factories depositing cinders - half an inch each year - caused the closure of the tunnel and it ceased to be used from around 1800. The Duke had an alternative route for the coal boats via the newly built Rochdale Canal, and Shooters Brook has since been culverted and diverted into surrounding sewers. The tunnel was then used for around fifty-five years to bring surplus water from the Rochdale and Ashton Canals into the Bridgewater Canal. It is interesting to note that the trustees of the Duke did not sell off the disused tunnel in 1879 because they saw its value as a possible part of a future underground railway.

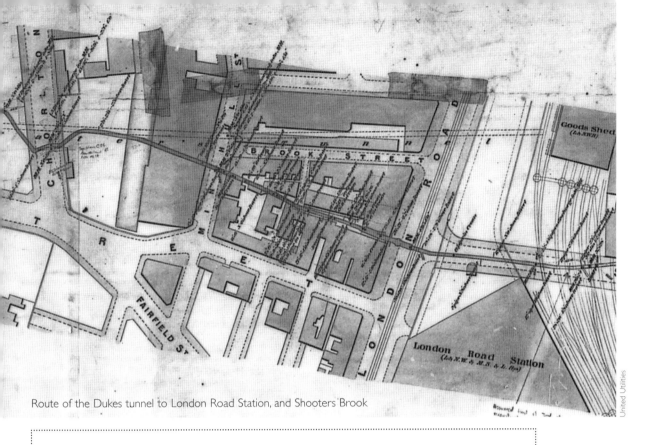

Route of the Dukes tunnel to London Road Station, and Shooters Brook

Garratt Hall

Much of the land beneath which the tunnel passed was the estate belonging to Roger Aytoun who owned Garratt Hall. The half-timbered building dated back to the fourteenth century when it was owned by the Trafford family.

Aytoun lived at nearby Chorlton Hall and had the nickname 'Spanking Roger'. He was a cavalry captain six feet four inches tall and came into great wealth by marrying the much older widowed Barbara Mynshull in 1769, and somehow managing to acquire sole ownership of the estate. He squandered much of the Minshull fortune and his distraught wife died in 1783.[4]

Manchester Archives & Local Studies

The estate contained orchards, dovecotes, and the fishponds, a pleasant area, half way along Shooters Brook towards Bank Top where people would take a Sunday stroll and buy flowers and salads. By 1841, some open land around Garratt Hall remained, but the surrounding area had completely changed with the rapid advancement of industry and housing, and the Brook had been culverted and built over.

Victoria Arches

The arches are situated under Victoria Street (previously known as Hunts Bank), in front of Manchester Cathedral. They are at the centre of many tunnel accounts in the city. These are the recollections of a *Manchester City News* writer in 1923 about the arches sixty years previously:

> 'I became acquainted with those arches in the sixties, for my father, a master joiner and builder, had a workshop there. Two approaches thereto were provided, one by the old flight of steps near the Cateaton Street side of the old churchyard, and the other at the corner of Victoria Street and Fennel Street. The arches were lofty and spacious, and had previously been used as a copper and iron works, in connection with which was a tall chimney by the Cathedral steps. Part of the chimney was damaged by lightning and the upper part was taken down in 1872, I believe, while the lower part remained till the old buildings at that point were demolished not many years ago'.

A Manchester Evening News letter in 1960 reveals more details:

> 'At the time I knew it well, 1898, one or two of the arches were used as a battery station by Manchester Electricity Department and two or three others as meter testing and storage departments. Also there was the first testing station for the department where the prototypes of all apparatus used by electricity users in the city were tested.
>
> The tunnel was bricked up about level with the end of Fennel Street. From its gradient it would reach approximately water level at the Irk at the bottom of Hunt's Bank and the other end would reach street level at St Mary's Gate. The roadway was one cart track wide. The entrance was in Victoria Street alongside the door to a tobacconist's shop near Cathedral Yard'.[1]

Manchester Archives & Local Studies

Joy Hancox

PLAN

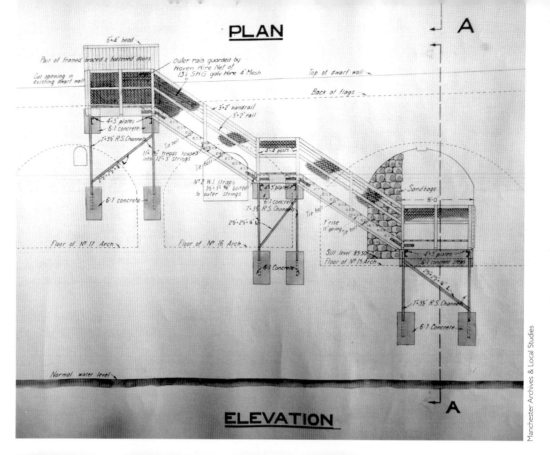

A

6×4' head

Pair of framed braced & battened doors

Cut opening in existing dwarf wall

Outer rails guarded by Woven Wire Net of 13's SWG galv Wire 4' Mesh

Top of dwarf wall

Back of flags

4×3 plates

6:1 concrete

7·3⅛" R.S.Channels

1½" t° treads housed into 12×3 Strings

3×2' handrail
3×2' rail

6:1 concrete

Tie bolt

Tie bolt

N° 2 W.I. straps 3½×½" bolted to outer strings

4×4' posts

4·5' plates

Sandbags

8-0

Floor of N° 17 Arch

Floor of N° 16 Arch

6:1 concrete
7·3⅛" R.S.Channels

2½×2½×¼"

7 rise
11" going

Tie bolt

Tie bolt

Sill level 85·50
Floor of N° 15 Arch

4×3 plates
6:1 concrete strips

2½×2½×¼" L

7·3⅛" R.S.Channels

6:1 Concrete

6:1 Concrete

Normal water level

ELEVATION

A

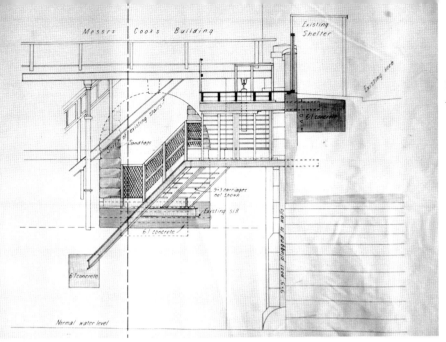

Drawings showing planned access to the arches from the river-side

Outside the arches, just below the Cathedral, was a landing stage where pleasure steamers took trips along the Irwell

The arches were used as an air-raid shelter during the last War. Planners estimated in 1939 that they would give protection for 3,500 people within ten minutes' walk of the shelters. There were to be three entrances along with access from the existing public conveniences adjoining the site. The final cost of the scheme was £10,150; two other entrances were added, and the revised capacity was dropped to 1619 people. It took about three months to convert the arches with additional brick blast walls. [2]

A suggestion was put forward the previous year, by the chairman, Mr Larrard, of the Air Raid Precautions Sub-Committee, for an emergency power supply. If the sub-station in the arches was put out of action then two men pedalling on a tandem with a dynamo would provide enough power to keep the ventilation fans going. People in the shelter would be asked to do half-hourly shifts. The chairman had seen wireless sets powered by this method in Central Africa. There is no record of the idea being carried out.

George Ainsworth remembers going down into the shelters during the bombing raids and described them as 'dirty old dungeons'. He didn't recall any seating for the fifty sheltering in his section of the shelter but remembered the cobbled surface. [3]

A sign in the shelter advised people to 'proceed in an orderly fashion'. An old police notice remains in place advising, in view of the mixed company taking refuge, that there was to be no smoking, insobriety, gambling, obscene language, rowdiness or unseemly conduct.

41

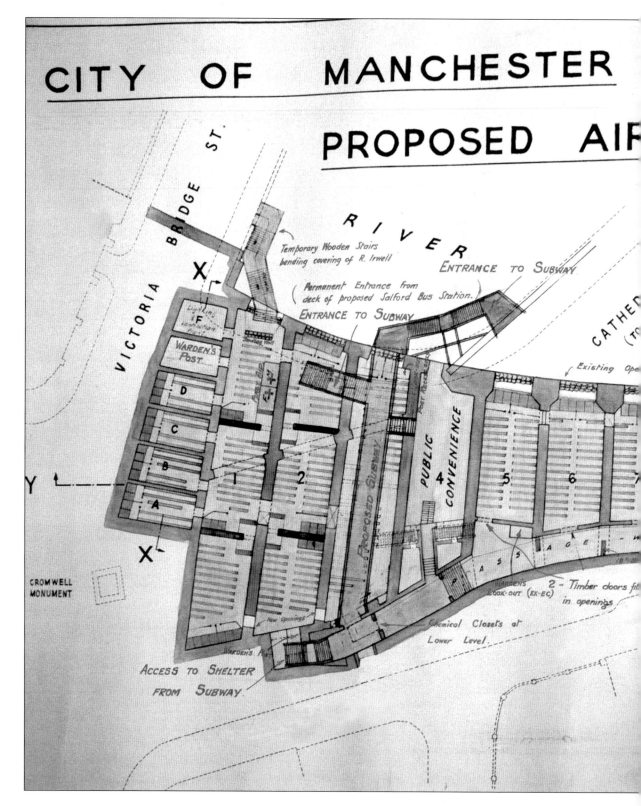

VICTORIA ARCHES

RAID SHELTER

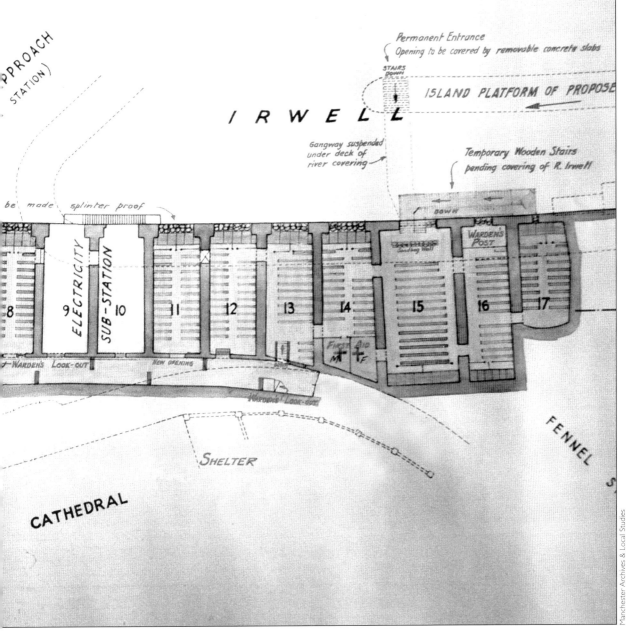

Permanent Entrance
Opening to be covered by removable concrete slabs

STAIRS DOWN

ISLAND PLATFORM OF PROPOSE

I R W E L L

Gangway suspended under deck of river covering

Temporary Wooden Stairs pending covering of R. Irwell

DOWN

— PPROACH
STATION)

be made splinter proof

WARDENS POST

ELECTRICITY SUB-STATION

8   9   10   11   12   13   14   15   16   17

WARDEN'S LOOK-OUT   NEW OPENING

First Aid M   F

WARDENS LOOK-OUT

SHELTER

CATHEDRAL

FENNEL S

When Ken Howarth went down into the arches for a Radio Manchester programme in the 1970s, he found many thin white stalactites and stumpy stalagmites, as well as an old safe and the lower part of a tramway gantry. This would have been one of Manchester's longest trolley-bus wire poles because it would have gone down into the floor of the arches a further 3 feet. Other surviving features included a 'drinking water' sign, the serving hatch of the canteen and a bricked-up entrance to an emergency escape passage which led to the junction of Victoria Bridge and Victoria Street.[4]

Manchester Archives & Local Studies

Toilet steps

joy hancox

Trolley bus wire pole

People also recall an old safe being found by council officials in the arches. It was not thought to have been there during war time and efforts were made to open it. Everything they tried failed, but when they looked behind it they discovered that its back had already been blown off. It was not known how a safe had been brought there, but it seemed someone wanted to force it open undisturbed. The safe may have belonged to Thomas Cook's who rented space in the arches.

The land covered by the arches included a street which led, at the west end, to a wooden bridge over the River Irk. There have been suggestions that the original houses are to be seen here, but it is actually just a series of seventeen arched spaces. Old prints show this was a sloping site. Many of the buildings here were badly built, and in 1814 several of them, along with a soap works, fell into the River Irwell, after their foundations had been undermined by water.

The old road had been covered over in an improvement scheme which began in 1833 and officially opened in 1839. There were problems during construction when the stone wall collapsed into the river in 1836.

The underground public conveniences next to the Cromwell monument, which stood on an island site opposite the cathedral, were closed in 1967.

Stalactites and stalagmites
in the arches

46

Passage way when the arches was used as an air raid shelter

The Cromwell statue prior to the building of the toilets. There was an underground route to Victoria Arches via the old landing stage from the premises of Thomas Cook.

RUTHERFORD
HOUSE

'Guardian' Tunnels

There is a tunnel network beneath the city code named 'Guardian', which was constructed in the 1950s to provide a secure telephone link between Manchester and other British cities and an installation in Scotland, in the event of an atomic attack. It came off the secret list in 1968 along with other exchanges - London's *Kingsway* and Birmingham's *Anchor* - when more details were released to the press. In 1999 BT stated the depth of the tunnel as over 200 feet, well below other foundations, which was at variance with figures quoted in previous sources.

In October 1968 it was visited by the Postmaster General, John Stonehouse, and details about the secret installation were made public. The exchange had cost four million pounds and had been operating for ten years. It was accessed by steps to a lift which took staff down 125 feet to the tunnels. They were protected from a nuclear blast by a thirty-five ton concrete slab door. Mr Stonehouse said that it had been 'the best kept secret in Manchester' , adding that 'this was extremely important for defence reasons'. The exchange was permanently manned by around fifty engineers, and extended 1000 feet beneath the city centre. It could be sealed in an emergency and had its own living accommodation, food supplies and fresh water well nearly 600 feet deep. Since it became operational in 1958 it had been handling ordinary trunk calls into the city, but this job had been transferred to the Rutherford Exchange. The underground exchange continued to connect trunk calls passing through the city. A GPO spokesman confirmed in 1968 that there were similar exchanges in London and Birmingham.

Manchester's bunker is in the city centre below buildings in Back George Street and George Street, with the 25 feet wide main tunnel between St Peter's Square and the Piccadilly Hotel connecting the two exchanges.

Pithead working near Piccadilly Gardens

Manchester Archives & Local Studies

The tunnel, which runs 1575 metres west to Salford, 978 metres east to Ardwick, and 900 metres to Dial House on Chapel Street, Salford, was built under strict government secrecy. Although it may have received some British Government financial support, the reported £4 million construction cost was mainly funded by the USA through NATO. Huge pithead towers went up near Piccadilly Gardens in 1954, with the official explanation that a GPO tunnel was under construction. There was much public speculation about the mining operation. Some thought they were digging for gold! During that period, office workers in the vicinity heard the explosions and felt the vibrations as the rock was cut through. Lorries bringing out the spoil used a huge ramp at the site. Although not officially confirmed, there were thought to have been several deaths during construction. There is also a newspaper reference to someone falling down the 100 feet deep lift shaft. The casualty was an inquisitive worker from an adjoining site who had plunged to his death after peering too far over the edge. [1]

The tunnel exits were placed outside the possible impact area if the centre of Manchester were hit. It is often repeated that non-English speaking workers were used so that they would not divulge what they were building. While it is true that the construction force was largely composed of Polish workers, it is not generally known that they were the remnants of the Polish Airborne Division who had served with the Allies and could not go back to their own country. In 1954 they were employed with other ex-servicemen on the project in, it is thought, a previously unworked underground area. Patrick Gouge was amongst the local workers employed there and one of the photos he took during construction was published in the Manchester Metro News in February 2002. In the 1950s, Patrick said that they were not told what the tunnels were for.

The real use of the building gradually filtered through to the construction workers, but as time went on it became clear that the shelters would not withstand the new Soviet 'H' bomb tested in 1955, which would have made a crater even deeper than the tunnel. Presumably as a response to this development, the Post Office Works Act and Bill were published 'to vest in the Postmaster General underground works constructed in London, Manchester and Birmingham in the exercise of emergency powers; and for purposes connected therewith' in July 1959. This confirms that Parliament would meet costs in maintaining the three tunnels.

While a certain amount of information is known about the tunnel through statements and news releases, and occasional visits by groups from other organisations, there is still an air of mystery about the workings. Manchester residents remembered that certain streets used to be cordoned off in the evenings to allow deliveries, with a police escort, into the tunnel. The full extent of the tunnels, their contents, activities and access points have yet to be made public.

In the event of an attack, staff in this underground village on two levels had six weeks of food rations. 'Guardian' had its own 574 feet deep artesian well - the same well which used to supply Boddington's Brewery. There were offices, a bar and welfare room along with rooms containing many bunk beds, kitchens, bathrooms, and two standby Crossley diesel generators known as Jane and Marilyn (after Jane Russell and Marilyn Monroe). It is said that there were teething problems with the generators and that the exhaust fumes caused the tunnel to be evacuated.

A standby generator

One visitor on official business in the 1950s was impressed by the shine and general smartness of the equipment. He also noticed the non-stop damp seeping through channels set into the walls. The canteen had an aquarium of tropical fish and in the mess room artificial windows with country scenes were painted on the wall. People who worked down there remembered the constant hum from the air-conditioning and fans, but if you walked out into the outer tunnels there was a deadly hush. The glare from the fluorescent lighting reputedly caused headaches and eyestrain. One apprentice employee whose job for six years was to replace the light bulbs in the tunnels described it as 'a horrible place' and was glad to get out. The main entrance shaft could be sealed by a thirty-five ton concrete slab which was lifted by hydraulic jacks.

The *Guardian* telephone exchange opened in December 1958, with the larger 'Pioneer' Trunk Unit with six test boards coming into service the following year and continued in operation until closure in the 1970s.

Many people have cause to remember the fire down in the tunnel in 2004 but this was not the first - there are newspaper accounts of trouble down below in 1969. The fire had been started by workmen in the new cable tunnel to Salford when they accidentally set petrol alight with a blowlamp. They beat out the flames on the blazing cables before alerting the emergency services. It took the fire services half an hour, wearing breathing equipment to move along the mile and a half smoke-filled tunnel to the source of the fire. The smoke was so thick that the overhead lighting made no impact. Manchester's Chief Fire Officer, Mr Harry Lomas, said the fire was one of the most unusual they had tackled for a long time and he praised the workmen who had 'kept their heads' and contained the fire until they arrived. Later it was confirmed that no calls were affected and that the cable had only been slightly damaged.

The following year further problems of extending the new cable tunnel link to Salford were reported. In an article headed 'FIGHT WITH FLOOD 130 FEET UNDER CITY', in 1970, the Manchester Evening News reported how a battery of water pumps had been pounding out a deafening roar 130 feet below Blackfriars Street in Manchester twenty four hours a day non-stop for the last eighteen months. This prevented the new GPO cable tunnel to the Dial House telephone centre in Chapel St, Salford from being flooded by millions of gallons of water that lay beneath the city centre. The pumps discharged three quarters of a million gallons a day into the River Irwell. Work was nearly complete on the link with the existing tunnel between Ardwick and Salford. Tunnel diggers worked round the clock for between £60 and £80 a week, in mud and water, to bore through the sandstone rock. It had been necessary to expand the tunnel because the trunk dialling system had become overloaded.

Today BT use it as a secure route carrying around 44 cables each containing 24 fibre optic cables which take thousands of calls simultaneously. In 2002 the decision was taken to refurbish the network of tunnels, including removing asbestos, and offer it for rent as storage or office space. But it was back in the news again on 29th March 2004, when the old exchange caused major disruption to the area. A fire down below badly damaged cable connections to the national network affecting 130,000 homes and businesses, and caused disruption to emergency 999 services. Greater Manchester and parts of Cheshire and Derbyshire were the worst hit. The blaze, near the junction of George Street and Princess Street, began at

3.20 am and was brought under control by 9 am. Automatic detectors alerted the authorities before more than 50 fire-fighters wearing breathing apparatus crawled 150 metres to the source of the fire. BT described the fire as 'very serious', with the reported cause being damage to 10 metres of electrical cables during work to remove asbestos, three days before the fire. It was fifteen hours before the intense heat and smoke had cleared sufficiently to allow telecom engineers to examine the damage. Roads in the city centre had to be closed off causing traffic chaos while the fire was tackled. It was said to have cost businesses an estimated £4.5 million.

There have been suggestions that the tunnel should be opened up as a tourist attraction - like the underground shelters at Stockport. One writer thought it could be used as a bar, a club or as a Cold War museum. The possibility of it being used in any of these ways is highly unlikely. Although some other centres of this period have been opened up to the public, BT seem keen to keep these tunnels secure because of the miles of cabling still in commercial use. They must have been concerned by the reports of a break in at the tunnels, just hours after the failed July London bombing attempts in 2005.

Intruders broke in at the Salford end and stole tools worth £14,000 and caused £20,000 damage. It was only discovered after BT received complaints from customers about problems with the service. A discarded cigarette end led to the conviction of one of the intruders. Since that incident, the Salford ventilated entrance building has been rebuilt and extra security fencing installed. At the Ardwick end, the previous building has been replaced with a lower ventilation block.

The now demolished exit buildings at Salford and Ardwick

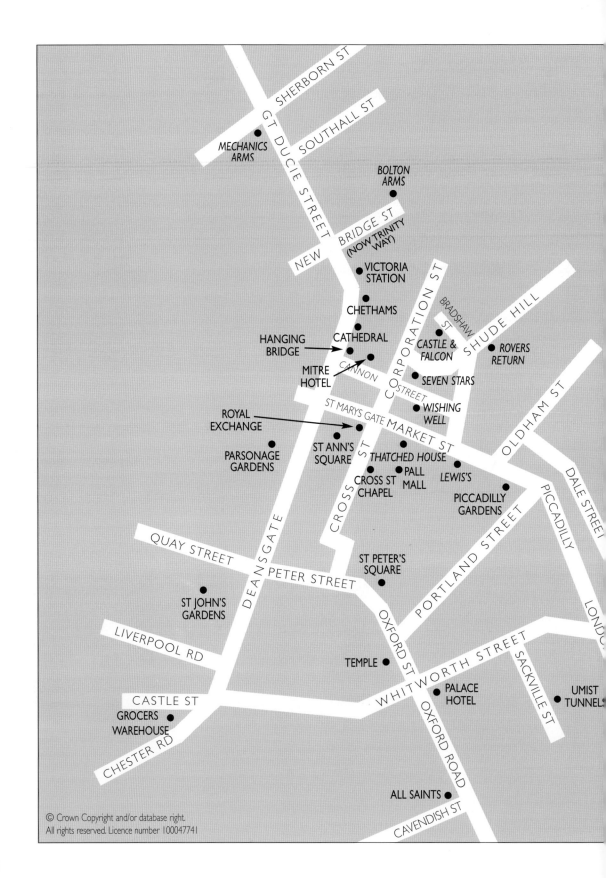

MECHANICS ARMS

SHERBORN ST

SOUTHALL ST

GT DUCIE STREET

NEW BRIDGE ST (NOW TRINITY WAY)

BOLTON ARMS

VICTORIA STATION

CHETHAMS

HANGING BRIDGE

CATHEDRAL

CORPORATION ST

BRADSHAW ST

SHUDE HILL

CASTLE & FALCON

ROVERS RETURN

MITRE HOTEL

CANNON STREET

SEVEN STARS

WISHING WELL

ROYAL EXCHANGE

ST MARYS GATE

MARKET ST

OLDHAM ST

DALE STREET

ST ANN'S SQUARE

CROSS ST

THATCHED HOUSE

PALL MALL

LEWIS'S

PARSONAGE GARDENS

CROSS ST CHAPEL

PICCADILLY GARDENS

PICCADILLY

QUAY STREET

DEANSGATE

PETER STREET

ST PETER'S SQUARE

PORTLAND STREET

LONDO

ST JOHN'S GARDENS

LIVERPOOL RD

OXFORD ST

WHITWORTH STREET

SACKVILLE ST

TEMPLE

CASTLE ST

GROCERS WAREHOUSE

PALACE HOTEL

UMIST TUNNELS

OXFORD ROAD

CHESTER RD

ALL SAINTS

CAVENDISH ST

St Peter's Church vaults

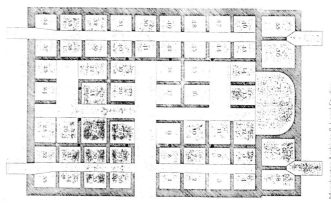

All Saints Church vaults

The City Centre

TER
EEL

FAIRFIELD STREET

Buildings and streets shown in italics, no longer exist

CAMBRIDGE DINING ROOMS

Rover's Return Shude Hill

All Saints

The 'tunnels' would have been the extensive church vaults as experienced by a group of impressionable youngsters by candlelight. All Saints Church in Chorlton-on-Medlock was consecrated in 1820 and had a large graveyard which was used until 1887 with around 16,500 buried there.

The church seated 1600 and was damaged by a blaze in February 1850, said to be have been caused by a fire to burn the Christmas decorations, which got out of control. Several weddings had been arranged for that day and some couples were married amidst the ruins surrounded by firemen, policemen and onlookers who had come to see the fire damage.

By 1938 part of the grounds had been made into council gardens and a children's playground. During the blitz of 1940, the church was hit beyond repair, and it was demolished after the war. In about 1949, 50 coffins were removed from the family vaults and placed together in a deep tomb. Rubble from the building was used to fill in the crypts and cellars, and many tons were taken away to strengthen the banks of the Manchester Ship Canal at Urmston. Some of the stonework was used by the sculpture students at the School of Art. The gardens at All Saints were completed in 1951.

ALL SAINTS TUNNEL

Thirty years ago I was an adventurous boy of 12. Standing where the park is now at All Saints was a church, in the grounds of which lay some very old gravestones. At one end of the grounds was a vault with steps leading down to two big iron gates. I and some pals decided to discover what lay beyond the gates. So one night, furnished with candlepower, we arrived at the vaults. The gates were not locked..... the tunnels all came to a sudden end. But in our tunnels (not all of them) were coffins of canons and noble people - no commoners. In recesses in the walls lay clay pipes, probably put there by workmen.

GBD   MANCHESTER EVENING NEWS 1967

Bolton Arms

Years ago I used to visit my mother-in-law who was in service with William Shakespeare Yates who owned the Bolton Arms at the top of Bridge Street. Often I went in the cellar, and I was told that a door led to Manchester Cathedral. The door (possibly rounded) had been whitewashed over. I believe that Mr Yates brought a surveyor to see it, and he advised him to leave well alone and not open it. Later the brewery bought the property from the Yates family.

DOROTHY T ELLIOTT   21 March 1973

The Bolton Arms, 83 New Bridge Street on the corner of Cross Street, Manchester had a bricked-up passage leading under the road towards Victoria Station. 24 January 1973 (JH)

Cannon Street

Thomas Cook had premises on Victoria Street opposite the Cathedral. The toilets referred to would have been across the road - underground. They reached the 'cavern' by means of steps down from Cooks into the Victoria Arches. (See plan and photograph pages 41 and 47.) Cooks seem to have used some of the underground area for storage. Mr Winter describes going north towards Cannon Street where there have been other references to a tunnel.

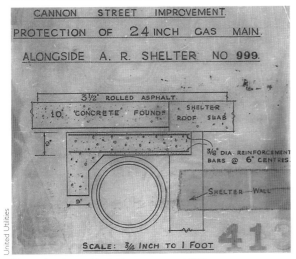

Records show that there were 1187 public air raid shelters in Manchester

WHEN I TRACED A TUNNEL UNDER THE CITY

Some 63 years ago I was an apprentice plumber, and worked in Cannon Street for a firm which did repairs to Thos Cook's booking offices, which were just a hut as seen from the street. But down below was a huge cavern formed by the passages from which the toilets were constructed. When we were there a brick wall was up to about two-thirds the height. The plumber I was with, got a ladder and we climbed over the wall and with our tallow dips, which plumbers used in those days, we explored the passages and estimated we were well on our way to ' Cannon Street and still no sign of an end.

G W   MANCHESTER EVENING NEWS 1967

During the Blitz, further up Cannon Street, opposite New Cannon Street. there was an underground shelter - number 999. The shelter in the former Wilton Hotel had a capacity for 200 people, but it was situated next to a twenty-four inch diameter gas main. Plans show reinforcement bars to make the shelter more safe. I wonder how many people seeking refuge there realized just how hazardous a site it was?

Castle and Falcon

As a child I lived at the Castle and Falcon pub on Bradshaw Street, just up from Victoria Station. During the war we would shelter in the cellar. There was a passage direct to the beer cellar, but on the left, there was a heavy door. We were told that there were cob-webbed skeletons behind the door and that the passage led to the cathedral. The pub (owned by Burtonwoods) was a lock up, and before that a church.
J JAMIESON-BLACK 1975 (JH)

There are reports of a man, held at the lockup in 1783, being led away to be hanged at Shudehill market. Two stained-glass windows survived from its former use as a chapel.

Chetham's

Tunnel accounts often refer to Chetham's, on Long Millgate, but there is no evidence of any underground routes except an old newspaper account of a passage to the Cathedral. The letter may refer to a well by the cloisters which is still in existence. People have claimed there is a ledge inside which could be part of a passage leading towards the Cathedral. It has not been investigated, and for health and safety reasons, the well has been sealed. The Cathedral authorities have not uncovered any evidence of a tunnel from Chetham's.

About 1842, a subterranean passage was unearthed at Chetham's Hospital in the small quadrangle which the cloisters enclose. It was believed to lead into the Cathedral. But I have never heard if the Cathedral-end of the passage has ever been discovered. But there can be no doubt that such a means of communication would be in use during the time the church was collegiated and the clergy lived in the adjoining buildings now known as Chetham's Hospital.
CITY NEWS 1915

An underground curiosity is mentioned in a Victorian guide to Chetham's. There is a description of the outline of a snake cut into stone in the floor of the cellar beneath a kitchen. This was said to be in memory of an incident involving one of the students and a snake, which is described in Mrs Linnaeus Banks' novel 'The Manchester Man'. Although there is a cellar traditionally known to Chetham's pupils as the 'Snake Pit', there is no snake drawing visible today.

Cross Street Chapel

United Utilities

An old City Engineer's drawing from around 1890 shows graves from the Chapel alongside sewers, pipes and mains, underneath Cross Street. Burials took place from the early 1700s until 1840. The 27 graves containing the remains of 100 people were exhumed in 1996 to be reburied in Southern Cemetery. Twenty-five years previously a much larger exhumation took place when 3000 bodies had to be transferred from the site of the old St James Church on Charlotte Street, for the building of St James' House.

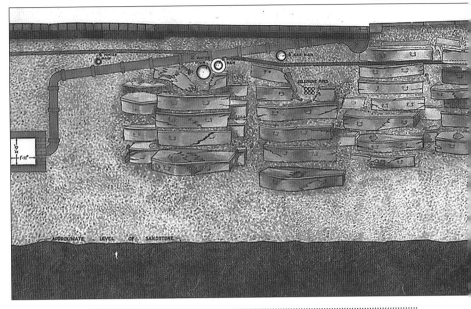

Dale Street Waterwheel

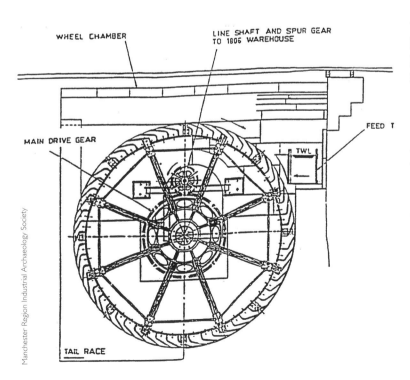

Manchester Region Industrial Archaeology Society

The remains of an old waterwheel have been found below ground, close to the Rochdale Canal at Dale Street which has been investigated by Manchester Region Industrial Archaeology Society between 1989 and 1994, after it had been rediscovered in 1983 by the Ashton Canal Society. The wheel, made with cast-iron and timber, was built in 1824 and worked inside an underground chamber, hoisting goods from the Rochdale Canal. The wheel is 15 feet 10 inches in diameter, and 6 feet 11 inches wide, it has 56 buckets and revolves at a speed of 8 rpm. Six years later it was extended by means of a 70 feet drive shaft below another warehouse. It remained in use until the late 1880s when it was replaced by hydraulic machinery.[1]

Grocers' Warehouse

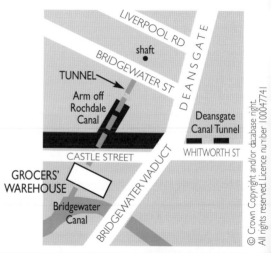

Coal from the Duke of Bridgewater's mines was transferred on the site from the canal to street level by means of machinery driven by a water wheel built by James Brindley. The coal was brought by boat in fixed boxes which were hoisted up a shaft - the first effective containerised transshipment of cargo. Cheap coal helped to establish Manchester as a major manufacturing centre. The transshipment tunnel went deep into the sandstone cliff. Plans show that it went as far as Bridgewater Street, although it may have extended further. This claim was substantiated during 2007 with the discovery, by historian Paul Sillitoe, of a shaft directly over the line of the tunnel on land being redeveloped between Bridgewater Street and Liverpool Road. This may have been used to haul up coal. The shaft was only briefly on view before the concrete foundations of a new building covered it. (see photo in 'Final Thoughts')

The Grocers' Warehouse was a later construction on the site. It was demolished in 1960 and the partial reconstruction was completed in 1987. Further demolition and development are planned along the line of the tunnel, and it is hoped that this will provide further opportunities to investigate the tunnel.

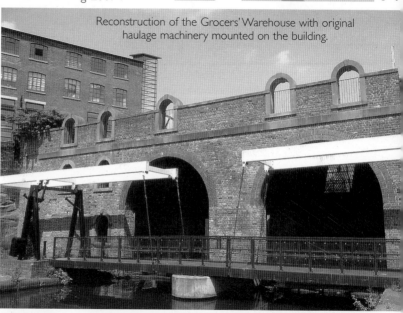

Reconstruction of the Grocers' Warehouse with original haulage machinery mounted on the building.

Harry Smith and team explored the tunnel, from the arm off the later Rochdale Canal, up to Bridgewater Street.

Arch in the tunnel excavated by Harry Smith

Hanging Bridge

The present bridge dates back to Tudor times and spans the ancient watercourse between Cateaton Street and Cathedral Yard. It was the main link between the town and the church but had been covered over. Building work in the late nineteenth century exposed the two arches, and it has now been incorporated into the Cathedral Visitor Centre.

In a hotel cellar in the vicinity of Hanging Bridge it was reported there was 'an entrance to an underground passage under the Irwell, possibly to Ordsall Hall. The owner had not gone down the passage himself, but the previous owner had, but had to turn back because of bad smells'. It is highly unlikely that the tunnel led under the River Irwell to Ordsall, but it may have linked to a route under Old Millgate. (See later chapter)

This was next to the Cathedral's burial ground - and in the past they were not so particular or respectful of the remains in graves. There are reports that in the early nineteenth century, when the old Church graveyard was completely full, in order to make room for new burials they had to dig up previous human remains - usually throwing bones into the River Irwell. Someone remembered seeing grave diggers carelessly throwing away bones - sometimes onto the footpath.

Human remains from the graveyard ended up in all sorts of unusual places. There was a great public out-cry when loaves appeared, stamped with a skull and cross-bones, from a discarded gravestone built into the floor of a baker's oven.[2]

Lewis's

The store on Market Street opened in Manchester in 1880 and was later noted for its underground attractions. The sub-basement had penny in-the-slot machines, distorting mirrors and Edison's phonograph.

Later they presented the first-ever concerts in a department store. Concerts lasted about thirty minutes and cost a penny to attend. The 'Penny Concerts' were a training ground for many artists.

Another basement attraction in the early 1900s was the re-creation of a Venetian scene. The public was taken on gondolas under the Bridge of Sighs along a 2 feet deep version of the Grand Canal to see the sights of Venice. The journey, which must have delighted many thousands of people, cost a penny and ended near the foot of a stone staircase which led unexpectedly and rather disappointingly, to the dismal reality of a street at the back of the store.[3]

Manchester Cathedral

There are several tunnel stories linking the Cathedral with halls and inns around the city. They mention entering via the crypt, but the Cathedral has not had a crypt since 1865 when problems with subsidence caused the church authorities to seal up the Trafford Vault. It contained nine coffins and memorial plates of members of the Trafford family, and George Tempest.

Below the base of the tower in the cellar are steps leading down to a bricked-up passage. It seems to go in a northwards direction and has been traditionally regarded by some Cathedral staff as a route to Kersal Cell. It is speculated that the passage caved in possibly because of its nearness to the River Irwell. The passage may have led to the River Irwell or into the Victoria Arches.

The Cathedral tower was taken down between 1862 and 1863. Two years later it was rebuilt in the hope that it would have a lofty spire, if funds permitted. At the start of the rebuilding in 1864, the chief cornerstone was laid by Right Rev James Prince Lee, first Bishop of Manchester, and a container of assorted coins was buried there.

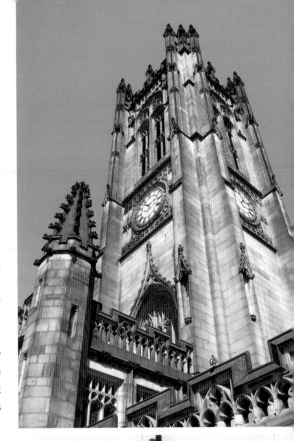

Mechanics Arms

The pub stood on the corner of Sherborne Street and Barker Street. There was a women's prison in the vicinity of the Mechanics Arms and there was a tunnel linking it with Strangeways Prison. I've heard mention of a bricked-up tunnel in the cellar of the Mechanics Arms.
STAN PARKIN 16 September 1971 (JH)

The pub was also reputedly linked by tunnel to Strangeways Prison: J BERRY in 1974 (JH) wrote:
'A tunnel runs to Strangeways Prison. This was done away with when some prisoners escaped about 15-18 years ago. You could see where the tunnel was. Two men were caught there.'

My parents went to see a large house on Teneriffe Street with a tunnel in the cellars which was said to lead to Strangeways. They did not buy it because of the tunnels.
MRS WINTER (JH)

Manchester Archives & Local Studies

During the Blitz, many other pubs in the area were completely destroyed. The Mechanics, so named because there were around a thousand people of that trade at the nearby engineering works, had all its windows broken and part of the roof blown off. Mrs Elsey, wife of the licensee, gratefully accepted the offer from the Governor of Strangeways of a cell for the night - naturally with the door unlocked!

The War destroyed the local 'rag trade' when the Mechanics used to sell salt herrings and black bread to the many Jewish employees in the area.

Mitre Hotel

The Mitre Hotel on Cathedral Gates has a tunnel which runs from south of the Cathedral towards New Cathedral Walk. The tunnel has eight side arches approximately eight feet deep. Facing the arches are the former windows of the hotel, suggesting that this was previously at street level. Those who rode to the services at the Cathedral would tether their horses outside the Mitre.

The hotel was originally known as the Old Church Tavern until around 1835. Prince Charles Edward Stuart reviewed his troops by the tavern in 1745. John Whitehead, the proprietor in 1817, was an ex-acrobat and, with some encouragement, would entertain the customers with a performance in the bar.

Palace Hotel

Beneath the three acre site is a lower ground floor and sub-basement. Here the benevolent employers of the Refuge Assurance Company provided a large staff dining room and fully fitted kitchens. The hall can also be used as a ballroom having a fully sprung floor, or as a theatre, complete with dressing rooms and orchestra pit. Refuge employees staged Gilbert and Sullivan operettas here and watched film shows. Conferences are now held in the carpeted ballroom. During the 1940s Blitz it was reinforced with extra iron-work to become a shelter for 1300 employees.

The building, still remembered by many as 'The Refuge', was built for the assurance company to the design of architect Alfred Waterhouse. The light and airy interior office space was regarded as revolutionary in its time. It was built in three phases, beginning in 1895 and completed in 1905.

It was once the site of Eagle Quay, which also stretched over the Palace Theatre land. As a basin off the Rochdale Canal, it was the terminus of a timber carrying service from Liverpool which began in 1824. Eagle, a new steam boat, pulled along other vessels carrying the timber to Manchester, where it would be sawn up into boards at an adjoining mill. The journey took over a day and cost 2s 6d per hundred feet of timber.

Parsonage Gardens

This was part of a two-acre parcel of land between Deansgate and the river Irwell owned by the Collegiate Church. In 1760 it was known as Parsonage Croft and it became the site for St Mary's church. Documents indicate that the builders of the surrounding houses had the right to drive tunnels or soughs, to carry water away into the river, providing it was not under the church or churchyard. The last burials took place around 1871 and it was stipulated, when the space was handed over to the Corporation as a public open space, that 'the human dust lying beneath should remain undisturbed'.

Piccadilly Gardens

The area was known from the sixteenth century as 'Daub Hole' through its use as a 'daub' clay pit for use in building. Deep holes formed, which became huge water pools. In 1755 the land became the site for a new infirmary and the holes were linked together to form an ornamental pond over 600 feet long and also to supply drinking water. It was renamed Piccadilly in 1812 as Manchester began to adopt London place names such as Pall Mall, Cheapside and Chancery Lane. The Infirmary on the site closed in 1909 and by 1920 the area was being cleared to build sunken gardens.

The old Piccadilly sunken gardens

An underground shopping centre for the gardens was proposed in 1963. The scheme for 104 shops, costing £1,250,000 was rejected by the planners, who thought it would be detrimental to the amenities of the area.

The site was approved for a nine-roomed 33,000 volt electricity substation 20 feet down which necessitated the resiting of the John Dalton statue to the Manchester Metropolitan University Dalton College, on Chester Street. The Lord Mayor, Mrs Yarwood, who opened the substation in July 1967, stated that not only was the substation the first of its size to be buried in Greater Manchester, it was possibly the first of its kind in the UK. Regulations stated that the roof had to be strong enough to take a bus or lorry running over it. Four thousand tons of earth had to be removed for the building, which replaced another underground station dating back to the 1890s.

Since 2006 a natural water source found 200 feet below the gardens has been used to supply the 180-jet fountain and to water the grassed areas. Heat generated from the substation caused problems to a newly laid lawn in the gardens in 2007.

Pneumatic Post

Details of the city's underground telegraphic service was given by Robert Johnson, the Postmaster of Manchester, at Withington Town Hall in 1889. Messages were propelled in an underground pneumatic tube system between Manchester Post Office at Spring Gardens and its branches at the Royal and Stock Exchanges, Hanging Ditch, Thomas Street, Mosley Street and St Peter's. Three pumps provided the air and there was speculation that in the future all mail would be transported by this method which in Germany, had been nicknamed 'the blow post'.

The pneumatic tube sent a cylindrical message carrier through a one and a half inch tube at a speed of 20 feet per second. The London Stock Exchange was the first to use this method, sending messages 220 yards to the Central Telegraph Office in 1853. The system was installed in other cities, including Manchester in 1865. By 1872 Manchester had a total length of 2,026 yards of lead pneumatic tube (compared to London's 12,800). The 451 yard link to the New Exchange used a larger two and a quarter inch diameter tube. The central engine station was at York Street,

There were proposals for a Manchester pneumatic railway in 1866 from Hunts Banks, and via Market Street to London Road Station. Pneumatic technology is widely used today, and the city of Prague still retains its own postal tube system.[4]

Rover's Return

Underneath the building were passages leading to the Cathedral and the river. John Chard, in an article in the *Valley Life Magazine* April/May 1988, writes *'One story I can verify regards the Old Rovers Retreat [possibly its name when a cafe] Shudehill, Manchester. As youngsters, a party of us were shown passages running under the building towards the Cathedral.'* (JH)

The pub is one of several in the city centre with passages reputedly leading to the cathedral. Situated on Shude Hill, it was said to be one of Manchester's oldest houses before it was demolished. Built in 1306 as the manor house for the Wythin Grave family, it became the Rovers Return in the nineteenth century. A sign outside claimed it was the 'oldest beerhouse in the City', and that Oliver Cromwell and Guy Fawkes reputedly took refreshment there. A fire badly damaged the premises in about 1928 and the licence was relinquished. Later, it reopened as 'the workingman's cafe' and was also used as an antiques shop.

Royal Exchange

Underneath the building in St Ann's Square is a service road and pavement, referred to as 'The Hovel' in a 1962 Manchester Evening Chronicle article. It was completed in 1921 and was still cobbled at the time of the newspaper feature. There was a turntable to return the vehicles back to the exit.

A recent eyewitness account described smaller tunnels at the far end running off in different directions including Market Street, but when I looked round the sub-basement, there was no evidence of any passages beyond the boundary of the building. However, there used to be

steps leading down from the sub-basement, but these have been covered over by parking spaces. Still visible, however are two large sealed entrances on the southern edge by the old kitchen area, one leading in the direction of St Ann's Street, and the other towards St Ann's Square.

The cobbles have been covered over and the turntable is not in use. The remaining section of the stabling has also been removed. It is possible that old passages were destroyed during restoration of the building, which was badly damaged by the IRA bomb.

Seven Stars Inn

The inn was situated on Withy Grove, and Frederick Tavare wrote to the CITY NEWS in 1892:

'...visitors may look for a key to the mysteries by descending to the cellars at the base of the old premises. Here at the present moment is visible an old arch, which is the reputed entrance to a secret passage which at one time is believed to have afforded subterranean communication with the old Collegiate Church, built in the fifteenth century (now the Cathedral), and thence, so tradition affirms, to the old Ordsall Hall, then the residence of the Radclyffes, a well-known Roman Catholic family. This secret passage, it is alleged, was, in the dim and distant past, not only made use of by the workmen at the Old Church, who received a penny a day for their wages, and got their dinners and other meals at the Seven Stars, but also played a prominent part in the escapades of the terrible Guy Fawkes, the never-to-be-forgotten hero of the great Gunpowder Plot, when, as the old ballad has it,

'Ye Papists did conspire
To blow up King and Parliament
With dreadful gunpowdire'

It is related that Guy Fawkes was concealed at the mansion at Ordsall. King James's soldiers were in close pursuit, and Guy Fawkes, reduced to the most pressing

The arch which may have caused the tunnel speculation

extremity, took to the secret passage, gained the Seven Stars, emerged into a room (still shown to visitors as Ye Guy Fawkes Chamber), darted through a still existing trapdoor in the ceiling, and by means of a gloomy passage, now utilized for spirits of another sort, gained the street and liberty. Mr W Harrison Ainsworth, Lancashire's novelist- historian, associates Guy Fawkes with the Seven Stars in one of his stories.'

Local historian T Swindells, author of 'Manchester Streets and Manchester Men' (1908) was not impressed by either the claims that the Seven Stars was Britain's oldest hostelry, or of a tunnel leading to the Cathedral. The ear-

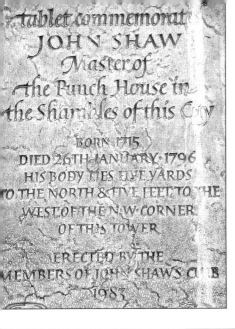

St Ann's Square

This was the burial ground of the church, which preceded the Cathedral and had closed by the 10th century. Some of the graveyard may have been removed with the building of St Ann's Church in 1712. There is no crypt at St Ann's but 600 people are buried in the churchyard. Burials ceased in 1854, and many of the gravestones were lowered below the surface of the pavement in 1892. Workmen digging a trench for an electricity cable in the Square in 1965 came across a human skull and bones, thought to be from the old churchyard. The Electricity Board re-routed the cable to avoid the burial ground. An unusual plaque on the church gives directions on how to find the now hidden grave a few feet away of John Shaw, the celebrated owner of a punch house in the former location of Sinclair's Oyster Bar.

St John's Gardens

More than 20,000 people are buried here, in the former site of St John's Church. Amongst them were John Owens, founder of Manchester University, and William Marsden, campaigner for the Saturday half holiday in Manchester which began in 1843. Their names are on a monument in the gardens. The church was demolished in 1931 and the grounds given to Manchester Corporation.

liest licence for it as a public house was 1551; before that date anyone could sell ale providing they could offer two beds and that they displayed a sign of a hand to indicate they had a barrel on tap. Records indicate that the Seven Stars was granted its first licence in 1356. Some have suggested that the Rovers Return, a short distance away, was older and that the builders of the Seven Stars took refreshments at the Rovers.

As for a tunnel, he states quite simply 'This is all myth. No such tunnel exists'. Whether or not there was a tunnel here previously, there was clearly no evidence of it in the early 1900s.

Swindells acknowledged that the inn was an interesting old place and worth a visit. In particular he mentioned the sad story behind a horse-shoe nailed to a post at the foot of the stairs. In 1805 a farmer's servant had been passing along Withy Grove leading his horse which had lost its shoe. He was holding the shoe as he passed by the inn, but at that moment a Press Gang who were staying there rushed out and detained him to serve in the army to fight Napoleon. Before he was forcibly taken away, the servant asked the landlord to nail up the horse shoe, which he promised to collect on his return from the wars. We do not know of his fate but the horseshoe was never reclaimed.

The historic Seven Stars, which had been under threat of demolition since 1899, was finally demolished in 1911, despite the protests of Swindells and others.

St Peter's Square

The square was the site of St Peter's church which was consecrated in 1794, seated 550 people and was designed by James Wyatt, one of the leading architects of his generation. Heaton Hall is the only other surviving example of his work in the area.

By 1906, the parish population had fallen from 3000 to around 300, and so it was decided that the building should be demolished. The church did not have a graveyard but had vaults and so when the city council purchased the site for £20,000, they eventually decided that the 46 vaults should be sealed up without interfering with the bodies, and a record made of the names of those who were interred there.

As the demolishers got down to the foundations, in 1907, they found a honeycomb of passages with coffins piled up on shelves.

Manchester Archives & Local Studies

It was clear that every available space had been filled and that the coffins were close to the floor of the church. Many prominent Manchester citizens were laid to rest here. The extensive vaults described as 'practically a catacomb' caused general surprise. Workmen also found a brass plate and coins and tokens encased in the wall from the time when it was built. The well-preserved tablet confirmed that Wyatt was the architect and that the foundation stone was laid in 1788.

A stone cross by Temple Moore, unveiled in 1908, marks the site of St Peter's Church within the memorial garden scheme which was dedicated in 1949 and designed by LC Howitt. The garden incorporates a stone cenotaph with the figure of the Unknown Soldier designed by Sir Edward Lutyens in 1924.

The Temple

Formerly known as 'The Temple of Convenience' because of its previous use as an underground public toilet. The pub on Great Bridgewater Street, with a standing capacity of around 55, opened in 1997 and is a favoured meeting place for artists and musicians.

Thatched House Pub

The premises on New Market Place were used as pub and post office dating back to the seventeenth century. Originally fronting on to Market Stead Lane, which became Market Street, the building is depicted in an old inn sign with a thatched roof and market stalls in front.

In the vaults there were a number of tunnels dug into the soft sandstone rock. They were said to lead in the directions of the Cathedral and Spring Gardens. Mr and Mrs Day, the publicans in the 1960s, were aware of the tunnels but had not entered them. The pub, a popular gathering place for Evening News and Guardian staff, was demolished in 1972 to make way for the Arndale Centre. (JH)

River Tib

The names Tib Street and Tib Lane in central Manchester remind us of the presence of one of Manchester's 'lost' rivers under the city. The description 'river' is misleading for a waterway which is little more than a stream or brook. 'Tib' is thought to be derived from the Celtic 'watercourse'. It was not always easy to find the waters, even before it was culverted. Tim Bobbin, the Milnrow writer, complained that he could not find a drop of water, except some purple liquid pouring out of a dyehouse.

The Tib rises in Miles Platting, near Collyhurst Street, and enters the city centre at New Cross, and passes under Tib Street, which was once the footpath beside the waterway.

A resident on the street in 1850 recalled that in the lobby there was a trap door covering the river. When it was raining, the rushing Tib below was noisy. At other times locals would throw their rubbish into the waters which would cause flooding in New Cross. Tib Street is remembered today for the many pet shops, and it has been immortalised in Howard Spring's 'Shabby Tiger' (1934).

At Market Street, in the 1700s, flag stones were laid across the Tib for the benefit of pedestrians. Just beyond here the scene was once described as '... a cluster of pleasant homesteads along its unculverted banks'. Much of the Tib was culverted in 1783, and it flowed in the direction of West Mosley Street and then towards Tib Lane, once a busy thoroughfare occupied by fustian dyers making use of the water.

The culvert had to be opened nearby at Cooper Street around 1850, when a policemen thought he heard someone shouting for help through a grid. A large hole was dug but the voice had come from a ventriloquist hoaxer on the street! [5]

The Tib flows under the Town Hall, the Extension, Central Library and the Midland Hotel. In 1787 it emerged from the culvert through open fields before entering the River Medlock near Gaythorn Bridge. Culverting of this section took place in 1820, and it was hidden beneath the site of Gaythorn Gasworks.

The Tib had been the boundary of Roman settlement at Castlefield and many objects, including a red urn from that era, were found at Gaythorn. The river, once an important source of drinking water, and a carrier of water to other parts of the city, deteriorated into a dumping ground, not only for residents but also for the mills and factories on its banks.

Surface water is now directed away from the culvert into sewers and drains, except at times of heavy rain when it can still cause flooding in the basements of some city centre buildings.

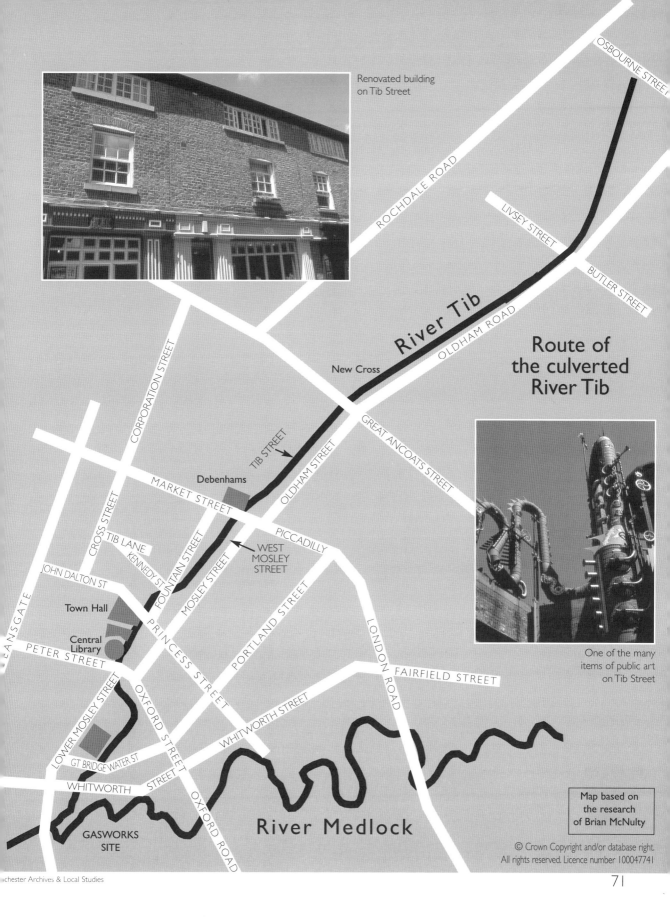

Renovated building on Tib Street

OSBOURNE STREET

ROCHDALE ROAD

LIVSEY STREET

BUTLER STREET

River Tib

OLDHAM ROAD

New Cross

Route of the culverted River Tib

CORPORATION STREET

TIB STREET

OLDHAM STREET

GREAT ANCOATS STREET

MARKET STREET

Debenhams

CROSS STREET

TIB LANE

KENNEDY ST

PICCADILLY

WEST MOSLEY STREET

FOUNTAIN STREET

MOSLEY STREET

JOHN DALTON ST

Town Hall

PORTLAND STREET

LONDON ROAD

Central Library

PRINCESS STREET

DEANSGATE

PETER STREET

FAIRFIELD STREET

One of the many items of public art on Tib Street

LOWER MOSLEY STREET

OXFORD STREET

WHITWORTH STREET

GT BRIDGE WATER ST

WHITWORTH STREET

OXFORD ROAD

GASWORKS SITE

River Medlock

UMIST

The Joseph Whitworth foundry once stood on part of what is now Whitworth Street. During the construction of the buildings for the Municipal Technical School of Technology, which opened in 1902 opposite the foundry site, mysterious dry brick wells were found eight feet in diameter and about 90 feet deep. They were confirmed to be annealing pits for big guns made here. The pits would be filled with oil and heated, then gun barrels lowered into them and toughened by gradually reducing the heat. Engineers working on the former UMIST site in around 1969 came across a five-acre network of passages and circular caverns thirty feet below ground. They were discovered during preparation for building construction beneath a car park between Sackville Street and Princess Street near the railway line. Research found them to be 200 years old. The caverns were about 7 feet in diameter and linked to passages 12 feet 6inches in diameter. They formed an underground reservoir system, taking water from the river Medlock, possibly for nearby mills. Engineers had the difficult job of locating and mapping the whole tunnel network in order to fill them with cement.

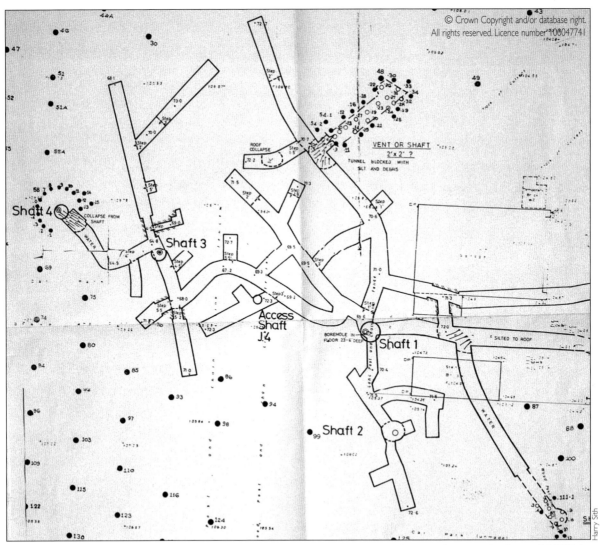

Network of tunnels found on the former UMIST site

Victoria Station

Three tunnels were discovered in 1972 underneath Victoria Station close to the present entrance to the car park on Long Millgate. They were found during test borings for the proposed Picc-Vic Tunnel near Millgate by number one platform, which was known as the Fish Dock.

Entry was down a concrete 16 feet shaft to a wooden platform. This led to passages which had been mostly backfilled with debris during extensions to the station. However, exploration revealed three tunnels leading down from Long Millgate towards the River Irk. Traces of coal were found, along with two cast-iron slewing plates, in one of the chambers. It has been suggested that minerals were transported here by tub or sledge from mines at Ardwick or Collyhurst.

Victoria Station is built over the River Irk on a raised platform and some of the original buildings remain below. The passages were possibly cellars or store rooms belonging to the mills built here between 1800 and 1830, as indicated on earlier maps. The brick arched passages, still in good condition, could have been used to transport goods to and from the river - possibly coal to power the mills. One of the sandstone pillars had rope-mark grooves suggesting that goods may have been hauled along here. Further research on the tunnels is not possible because the inspection chamber has been flooded and sealed.

Another tunnel is known from Old Millgate, opposite Hanover Street which led down to the Irk. A 1792 deed shows a watercourse which linked with the river.

Twenty feet below the station is the old bridge over the River Irk which linked Long Millgate with Walkers Croft. The bridge is still in use, although its sides are covered over, and the sound of the river going over a weir can be clearly heard.

Bridge over the River Irwell

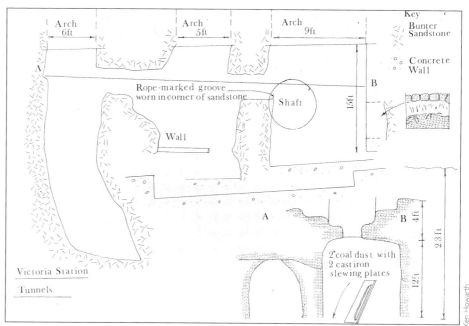

Three tunnels under Victoria Station

Undercroft between Aspin Street and Reed Street

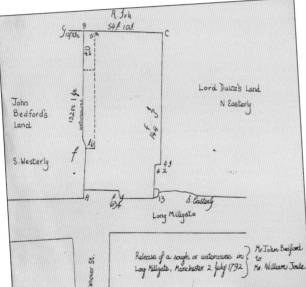

1792 document showing
watercourse off Long Millgate

British Rail engineer examines the tunnel wall

Manchester Local Studies
Librarian, Chris Makepeace
with the slewing plates

Ken Howarth

Manchester Archives & Local Studies

In the archway space under the station there is a large block of sandstone around 30 feet long which the builders did not remove, but worked around. Also still to be seen are steps up to a reputed entrance of the old Walkers Croft graveyard, and the bricked-up door to a subway which went northwards under the platforms. Excavations for the subway went through the graveyard where the coffins were left in situ. In 1847 people standing on the platforms complained about the unpleasant smell coming from the graveyard, below. Coffins and skeletons from the graveyard which was used up to around 1832, have been found at various times during maintenance work at the station. In around 1950 work was stopped while several square-shaped coffins were examined. They were made of mahogany and in a good state of preservation and were later covered over with concrete.

There used to be a coal chute between two of the platforms on the main concourse. Coal was then taken in handcarts to the boiler house.

Excavations in 1993 revealed a huge Second World War bunker under the station. The concrete cavern 50 feet down was an emergency communications centre.

Sandstone

It was situated under platforms fourteen to sixteen and came into use in December 1940 when a large portion of the western end of the station was bombed. Thirty-six people manned the cramped and badly ventilated control centre until a new, better-equipped, room was provided in the Hunts Bank building in 1942.

Installations below the station

The River Irk beneath Scotland Bridge

Reconstruction of the Spring Gardens conduit at the 1887 Queen Victoria Jubilee exhibition at White City.

Wells

While building an underground car park in the vicinity of Pall Mall in 1959, workmen found the remains of an old well 26 feet below street level. The shaft was around 3 feet in diameter and 17 feet deep. The upper part was in stone and it flared out to 4 feet in diameter into the rock. Amongst the rubble in the well were two timber water pipes. They appear to have been part of a valve about 10 feet from the bottom.

One of Manchester's earliest sources of drinking water was a spring near the corner of the present King Street and Spring Gardens. It was known as 'The Fountain' around 1650, when there were other wells at Shude Hill, Withy Grove and Castlefield. The quality of the water was called into question in 1711, when a report described it as '...in general hard and impure. It is impregnated with a large quantity of selenite and contains no considerable portion of alum ... one observation that the inhabitants of this place are peculiarly subject to glandular obstructions and scrophulous swellings and that water, loaded with stringent and earth salts hath a direct tendency to produce such complaints'.

Residents in this fashionable area were forced to sink further wells as supplies diminished in around 1776. When Manchester's first Theatre Royal was being pulled down in 1868, workmen came across the original well under the stage area, with water still to a depth of around 16 feet. **6**

Wishing Well Cafe

The basement restaurant known as 'The City Restaurant' was on the corner of New Brown Street and Cannon Street. It was renamed after a shaft was discovered under the floorboards by an electrician in around 1954. The management decided to make a feature of it and opened up the floor to construct an imitation well. A few bones were found in the well, and so a skeleton was displayed next to it for dramatic effect.

The restaurant was a popular late night venue and at weekends it became the Cord Disco, named after the owner's American car. New Brown Street for a time was locally known as Manchester's Carnaby Street, with its fashionable clothes shops.

Prior to the demolition of the site to make way for the Arndale Centre shopping development in 1973, Harry and Dick Smith and the restaurant owner, Alex Britton, worked to clear the debris down to 75 feet from the well shaft. Nothing of consequence was found in the rubble - just pieces of broken pottery, animal bones, old hooks and demolition material from a previous building. Part way down they found a large chamber - possibly a storage bay for coal, and a ledge for candles. There were burnt timbers here and it may have been part of an airshaft, and could have connected with other workings.

The excavators thought that the 8-feet wide, brick-lined well shaft with holes cut into the sides to support ladders was more likely to be a coal or copper mine. There were said to be similar workings at Shude Hill and Corporation Street. However, early maps show a number of wells around the city, including in nearby Market Street, and experts say it was not uncommon for wells to have a chamber at the bottom. Harry and his team came across a larger, lower chamber and they needed longer on the dig to try to solve the mystery of the well. Another problem was that they were running out of storage space in the building to store the excavated rubble. Further time extensions were not granted and the shaft was refilled to disappear under the Arndale Centre. They estimated that they were still possibly 40 feet off the bottom of the shaft.

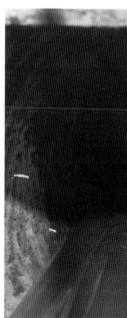

Alex Britton (left)
with Harry and
Dick Smith

Harry Smith wrote of the excavation:

*We had three months to empty and clear it out. ... it was 10 feet deep
at the time. I went down to have a look at it; the lining looked very
strong and thick for a well and the infill was full of building rubbish.*

*My brother and I hired a barrow hoist and made a big tipping bucket.
We got very good at free wheeling the bucket down the shaft without
dropping it on the bottom. After about a week of digging, we came
across a large tunnel. It took four days to clear it out of rubbish.
It turned out to be a large storage chamber. After another few feet
of shaft clearing we hit water, and we hired a three inch pump.*

*We had to keep a small sump ahead of digging to keep the water
down. After the pump was installed it never stopped running ... One day
we had gas in the shaft and could not breathe, so we installed a fan
and the output was blown into a plastic roll, as drawing this could then
be put further down the shaft without having to stop work to lengthen
the end further down the shaft. All the way down the shaft were liner
holes in the wall to take 8" x 8" timbers, making a small staging. When
we got to eighty feet we were told we would have to leave the site.
By now we had worked every day for three months and still pumping
a lot of water. We had to give up without finishing the work. After
working out the amount of water pumped out, we decided there must
be a big area open at the bottom of the shaft.*

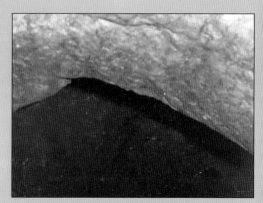

The roof of the lower chamber

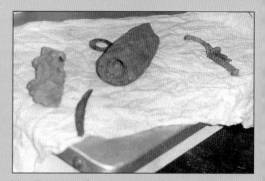

Metallic objects found in the shaft

Looking down the shaft

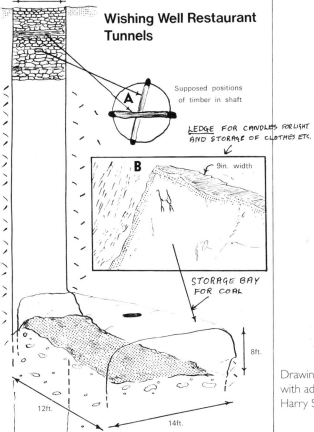

Wishing Well Restaurant Tunnels

Supposed positions
of timber in shaft

LEDGE FOR CANDLES FOR LIGHT
AND STORAGE OF CLOTHES ETC.

9in. width

STORAGE BAY
FOR COAL

8ft.

8ft.

12ft.

14ft.

Harry Smith at the Wishing Well

Drawing by Ken Howarth
with additional notes by
Harry Smith

Old Millgate
and Market Place

New Cathedral Street is a major new thoroughfare in the city and is on the site of Old Millgate and Market Place. Mancunians once flocked here to wander around the market, the old pubs and food shops and also to visit its underground attractions. A 1937 Manchester Corporation guide described it as an area where 'a charm awaits the visitor at every corner's turn'. Beneath these streets there is evidence of a tunnel running from the direction of the cathedral towards Market Street and Deansgate. The following 1929 *Manchester Guardian* article speculates about the mysteries of the underground area here:

'Few of the thousands who daily hurry along Corporation Street and Market Street are aware that beneath their feet are centuries-old passages, honey combing that area of the city, and into which, on occasions, workmen have fallen. If, as is possible, the block of buildings lying between the two streets is pulled down or set back by its recent purchasers, it will be interesting to see what is brought to light by the uncovering of a passage which apparently runs from the Cathedral towards Piccadilly. As to its age and its original use, one can only make guesses.

Part of it can be entered from Walmsley's shop, which has been used continuously as an outfitters for nearly 140 years. And even before that came into being the site was occupied by houses, the cellars of which, fitted with ranges, were not only used as habitations by certain unfortunates, but also formed entrances to the passage. So it must be quite venerable. Some say that it was built as a sewer to the river, some say its obvious use was for storage, but romantics visualise this and all underground passages as elaborate 'funk-holes' for less peaceful times. By connecting the habitable cellars and the roomy passages together it is possible to think of them being used exclusively by a mysterious section of the people who lived a remote and subterranean existence out of the sight of their more normally housed fellows. Cooking and sleeping in the cellars, roaming along the passages, they most certainly played skittles in that queer underground skittle-alley beneath Market Place, where now fragrant cheeses are stored.'

Top: Market Place and Old Millgate
Left: New Cathedral Street

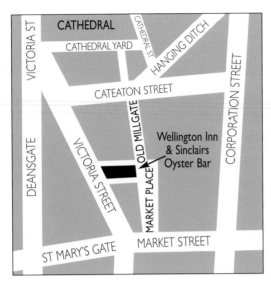

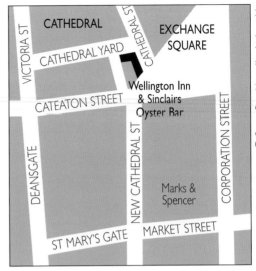

Left: Market Place and Old Millgate before redevelopment in the 1970s.

Right: Present day plan with new thoroughfare New Cathedral Street.

To fit alongside a 1974 development, the Wellington Inn and Sinclair's Oyster Bar were raised nearly five feet as part of Shambles Square. Following the IRA bomb damage to the area in 1996 and further redevelopment, the inns were taken down and rebuilt in a new location at Cathedral Gates. They re-opened in the new 'L'-shaped formation in 1999.

Walmsley's shop, described as a point of access into a passage between the Cathedral and Piccadilly, would have been 'Walmsley Brothers' hosiers at 27 Market Street. Although the route is known to the writer he does not seem to have ventured down there. The article also refers to the cellar dwellers who led strange subterranean lives. In 1836, there were an estimated 18,000 living in cellars, in Manchester. Reports in the 1830s and 1840s revealed the shockingly overcrowded and insanitary conditions of the cellar homes. They were often regarded by the rest of the population as places of conspiracy and disease, but the occupants did not spend all their lives underground; they would have worked in mills and factories. Many of them were Irish immigrants who started out in this cheap accommodation. [1]

Celllar dwelling

82

Journalist, George Mould mentions the skittle alley below Market Place, and other delights:

> 'It was a warren of narrow streets in which was an amazing collection of licensed premises. Best known perhaps was the Bull's Head which housed a curious three cornered chair in which it was said Prince Charles had sat when he made his headquarters there when he reached Manchester during the 1745 rebellion.
> (Most of the pubs) ... supplied sandwiches, some of them supplied luncheon. At midday they were respectable enough - merchants from the Royal Exchange across the way crowded into them. At night they attracted a very mixed crowd. The narrow passage ways were an attraction to some pretty sleazy customers and many a cotton man delaying his homeward journey for a 'quick one' stayed longer than he should and came round to find himself with a hangover and no wallet! The shops in the area were a joy. There was one which specialized in vintage China teas. There was an ancient underground skittle alley where rare cheeses were stored.' [2]

Manchester Archives & Local Studies

A photograph of the Old Market Place in the late 1890s, shows on the left, the lamp above the entrance to the underground shooting range and skittle alley which later became a cheese store.

Manchester Archives & Local Studies

An 1892 report in the City News describes an interesting find in the passage below Old Millgate:

> 'There is a rumour that some time since two skeletons and some ancient coins were discovered in the cellar (part of a passage) now occupied by a Mr Green, at No 2, Old Millgate, next door but one to the Falstaff Hotel.'

Long Millgate, where there was a newspaper report of a tunnel in 1899

Another report dated the coins as being from the sixteenth century. A *City News* article in1899 is the first specific reference to the skittle alley beneath a public house. It also indicates links to another part of the city.

> 'Underneath the pavement in Old Millgate, on the right-hand side, is a long tunnel at present used as a skittle alley in connection with the public-house, 2a, Old Millgate. The proprietor informs me that this is part of a subterranean passage running from the Cathedral. The tenant of 57, Long Millgate, informs me that a similar passage exists in the rear of his premises running in the direction of Red Bank.'

Market Place and Old Millgate c1936. Note the vertical Goulburn's sign

The premises on Old Millgate were occupied by Messrs Smith, Hill and Co, linen drapers. The proprietors had another shop on Cannon Street which was linked to it by an underground passage.[3] A *City News* article in 1924 claimed the business had been in Old Millgate for well over two centuries; but the same year they were bought out by the food purveyors, Goulburn's, who acquired most of the block from number 2 to 14, thought to date from 1850. They had a change of use for the space below the cellars:

> '...the old skittle alley now used as a cheese and egg storeroom, running underneath the whole block. This alley is walled off at each end with newer bricks, and it is found that it continues under the Smith Hill premises. Evidently, at the other end, it must have originally run as far as Market Street, unless it turned into the Bulls Head Yard.'

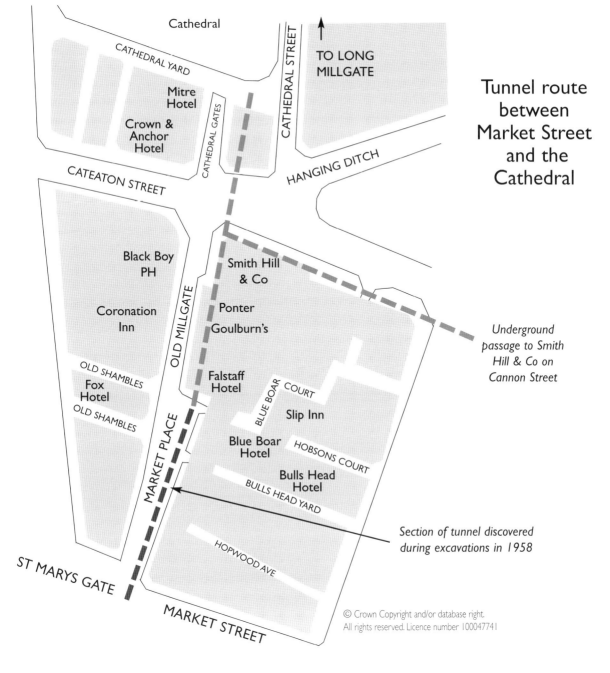

Cathedral

CATHEDRAL YARD

CATHEDRAL STREET

TO LONG MILLGATE

Tunnel route between Market Street and the Cathedral

Mitre Hotel

Crown & Anchor Hotel

CATHEDRAL GATES

CATEATON STREET

HANGING DITCH

Black Boy PH

Coronation Inn

OLD SHAMBLES

Fox Hotel

OLD SHAMBLES

OLD MILLGATE

Smith Hill & Co

Ponter

Goulburn's

Falstaff Hotel

BLUE BOAR COURT

Slip Inn

Blue Boar Hotel

HOBSONS COURT

Bulls Head Hotel

BULLS HEAD YARD

MARKET PLACE

HOPWOOD AVE

ST MARYS GATE

MARKET STREET

Underground passage to Smith Hill & Co on Cannon Street

Section of tunnel discovered during excavations in 1958

BERNARD WEBSTER, who had been into the tunnels, was interviewed in 1972 (JH), and reported that there were two levels below. The lower one, known as the cheese alley, had previously been used as a skittle alley and also for archery. The 3 feet circular target holes for the archers were to be seen. The alley was towards the front of the building and ran in a north-south direction. Mr McHugh, in charge of the bacon and ham at Goulburn's, took Bernard Webster into the tunnel, and claimed it connected with a passage from the cathedral. There was also a well or water storage in the tunnel, which had been covered over. Bernard Webster emphasized that these passages were neither cellars nor sewers. From his experience as an employee for Manchester Council in the Planning and Engineers Department for nearly twenty years, he already knew the location and route of the sewerage system. He described the tunnel as built before 1820, and 6 feet 6 inches in height.

GEORGE BELL was fifteen when he was employed by Alfred Goulburn:

> 'At the corner going towards Kendals there was a wooden hoarding which had been there about fifty years. The boss told me to pull it down, and behind I found a door and stone steps running down from it to a tunnel. There were spears and shields and I killed about thirty rats. We found the passage ran to the Cathedral. Curators from a museum came and took the spears away. We turned the tunnel into an egg-testing station'.
> 1974 (JH)

THOMAS A TAYLOR lived in Hulme, and at the age of eight he used to go with an older friend on his mineral drinks delivery-round. His description seems to indicate that there were passages linking Goulburn's with other establishments.

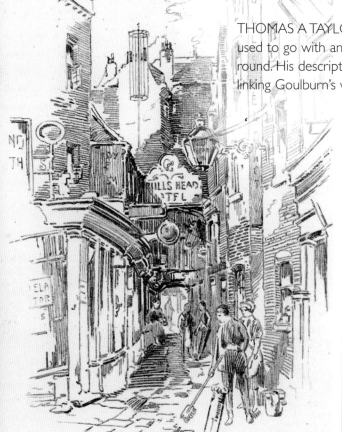

> 'One of the first stops, I well remember, was the Bulls Head Hotel just off the Shambles. Inside the pub down the cellar steps while John (his friend) was stacking the mineral boxes on the side of the wall that seemed to be like a tunnel, I wandered further on.
> The walls were brick, the ceiling was semi-arched, and I well remember passing some cheeses.
> I went on and on then became frightened.
> I turned back but could not find my way out again. I realised that the passages were not straight, but honey-combed, going in all directions like a maze. John found me, and said 'Where have you been?' But when you are young you seem to make light of incidents at the time.'
> (JH)

Joy Hancox

Goulburn's underground cheese store

SPECIALLY PACKED
FRUIT
FROM THE
IMPERIAL FRUIT SHOW
LONDON

THE PREMIER WINNING EXHIBITS
FROM THE IMPERIAL FRUIT SHOW
CRYSTAL PALACE
SHOW AT GOULBURN'S IN
"YE OLDE SKITTLE ALLEY"
NOVEMBER, 1922

Joy Hancox

Goulburn's display referring to the skittle alley

An *Evening Chronicle* article of 1958 could quite possibly refer to another section of the tunnel which ran under Goulburn's.

A mystery, below-surface passageway was uncovered by demolition workers near the corner of Market Street and Market Place - centre of 'old' Manchester.

I clambered in through the opening; peering into the half-light, breathing the cold, clammy atmosphere of yesteryear. Most of the brickwork in the 9 feet high, 5 feet wide tunnel was flaking with age. It stretched for about 25 yards, crossing below Market Place. There it had been bricked off. An official of the main firm handling the work said: 'There is no sign of this passage on the plan from which we are working. The tunnel seems to run in the direction of the cathedral. It may even have been connected with it.'

Later, when the site for the Arndale Centre was being cleared for construction, workers discovered another tunnel running under Corporation Street from the site of the present Marks and Spencers in the direction of Piccadilly.

MYSTERY TUNNEL IN CITY CENTRE

A MYSTERY, below - surface passageway was uncovered by demolition workers near the corner of Market Street and Market Place—centre of "old" Manchester (writes an Evening Chronicle reporter).

I clambered in through the opening peering into the half-light, breathing the cold, clammy atmosphere of yester-year.

Most of the brickwork in the 9ft.-high, 5ft.-wide tunnel was flaking with age.

It stretched for about 25 yards, crossing below Market Place. There it had been bricked off. An official of the main firm handling the work said: "There is no sign of this passage on the plan from which we are working.

"The tunnel seems to run in the direction of the cathedral. It may even have been connected with it."

Demolition of the Market Place site

88

Joy Hancox

Shambles in its original location in 1967.

An ex-Manchester fireman, NJ Wain, confirmed in 1974 (JH), that in the Shambles there used to be an entrance under Goulburn's fish and game shop leading towards Deansgate. Goulburn's achieved fame during the War when Sir Winston Churchill sent them a telegram requesting cheese. This was at a time of food rationing, but the Prime Minister's order was dispatched and the telegram was proudly displayed in the shop window.

The Market Place and Old Millgate area was devastated by enemy bombing in 1941. The site of over seven acres, bounded by Corporation Street, Market Street, part of Exchange Street, Deansgate, Cateaton Street and Cannon Street, was subject to a Compulsory Purchase Order in 1956. Excavation work the following year revealed the remains of the skittle alley below the Falcon Inn, along with an old well. Goulburn's, who had other branches in the Grosvenor Arcade and Edge Street, went into liquidation in 1964 after 117 years of trading.

By 1970 work had begun on a £10 million scheme, which at one stage had seriously considered a proposal to demolish the Wellington Inn and Oyster Bar, which had suffered war damage. It took a council vote of 107 in favour to 11 against, to reprieve the buildings, which were classified at the time as an ancient monument. So the old inn and bar became the only survivor of one of Manchester's most vibrant and interesting areas.

INTERESTING ANTIQUARIAN DISCOVERY
IN OLD MILLGATE.

W. G. PONTER

W. Has had the "CRYPT" Electrically Lighted and it is
NOW OPEN to the Public. Admission by Address Card.
The centre pillar and the beautifully groined roof are master-
pieces of the old builders' art.
The "Crypt" is approached by steps from an opening in the cellar
floor and is about 30 feet below the street level.

Photograph (top) of Ponter's
crypt taken in 1906 appears
to show excavations.

There was something else that was lost with
the combination of the Blitz and the excavation of the site. In 1903 an advertisement
appeared in a local newspaper inviting the
public to view the recent discovery of a
mysterious cellar under the property of W G
Ponter, furniture dealers and decorators at
20-22 Old Millgate. Described as a 'crypt' 30
feet below ground, it was accessed by steps
from an opening in the cellar. It was described
as having a 'centre pillar and beautifully
groined roof' and as 'masterpieces of the old
builders art'. As a final enticement to the public, the 'crypt' could be
viewed by electric light.

A newspaper article the same year speculates on the cellars origins:
*'A problem of interest to antiquaries is set by the discovery
under some business premises in Market Place of a cellar of
curious construction. It is a vault about six yards square, and
is a fine example of groining in brickwork. There is a short
stone pillar in the centre, and from it rise the arches in the
usual formation. There are also arches round the walls. The
workmanship is excellent, and it is fresh and well preserved.
There is no certainty as to the original purpose of the cellar.*

*Its appearance strongly suggests a crypt, but there is very
little to support the theory that the place was ever a crypt.
From the evidence of the brickwork it seems unlikely that
it is older than the beginning of the eighteenth century.
In 1730 or thereabouts a common standard in the size
of bricks was adopted. The bricks used in the construction
of the cellar are of varying size, and they are for the most
part smaller than those used after the middle of the
eighteenth century. Underground rooms arched in a similar
manner, only without the groining, have been unearthed
in several places in the immediate neighbourhood of the
centre of the city. This is certainly one of the best
constructed, and the excellent groining marks it out
among finds of the same nature.'* [4]*

The article then goes on to link the cellar with John Byrom's house.
However, maps indicate that his home was on the corner of
Hunters Lane and Hanging Ditch, and not directly over the crypt.
It is also known that his accommodation was rented and therefore
he was not in control of changes to the property, and so the
likelihood of secret meetings here between Byrom and other
Jacobite supporters has never been proved.

In the next chapter I uncover the evidence of an underground
network leading from Market Place and along Deansgate.

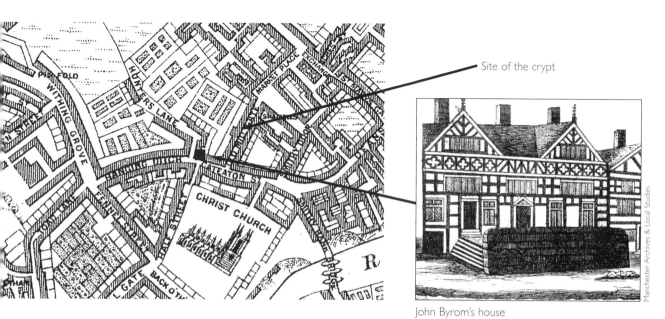

Site of the crypt

John Byrom's house

'I went into the tunnel and was told
at one point we were under
subway level at Kendals'

'the tunnel ... large enough
for a single-decker bus
to pass through'

Deansgate

One of the most intriguing things I have come across are accounts of a tunnel running beneath Deansgate between the Cathedral and Trafford Bar. This is not be confused with the well-documented Manchester and Salford Junction Canal tunnel, which runs under Deansgate at Camp Street. Nor is it the pedestrian subway which used to connect the Kendals stores on either side of the street. There are indications that the Deansgate Tunnel was of a substantial size, being described as large enough to accommodate a horse and cart or a single-decker bus. The evidence comes from a number of different sources all independently pointing to an underground route that very few people know of. I have talked to council employees, past and present, about this tunnel and a linking route towards the Cathedral but they are mystified. I should point out that such a route would be lower down than the utilities and therefore does not feature on the Council's extensive sewer records. The following accounts seem to be referring to the same route:

The *Manchester City News* reported the accidental discovery of the tunnel, just off Deansgate, in 1911. The article indicates that the brick-arched tunnel close to the John Rylands Library was thought to extend beyond the end walls and had been known about for at least fifty years.

'MANCHESTER MYSTERY A Subterranean Passage.
A wide field for speculation or research on the part of local antiquaries has been opened by a discovery which was made in Cumberland street, Deansgate, a few days ago. While workmen were engaged in demolishing some dwelling-houses there they came across an underground passage. It has an arched roof, built of brick, and is wide and high enough to allow a horse and cart to travel along it. Penetrating the passage, the men found that it extended for about seventy yards before being closed by a brick wall. There is evidence, however, to show that this wall does not mark the end of this underground way.

> *'the passage, if thoroughly
> explored, would be found to run
> from the river Irwell, near Water
> Street to another point close
> to the river near the Cathedral'*

Cumberland Street

The Deansgate premises of Thomas Armsrong and Brother which later became the site of the Houldsworth Hall. Armstrongs were opticians to the Infirmary and Eye Hospital and scientific instrument makers to the Goverment. They also supplied the present Cathedral clock.

An experienced builder, with whom a representative of the City News had a conversation on the subject, is of opinion that the passage is between 200 and 300 years old, and an old resident in the neighbourhood says that over fifty years ago he was aware of its existence. He states that when he was a boy he had been in it and in other subterranean passages in the district, so situated as to indicate that they are sections of the one that has now been brought to light. Indeed it is suggested that the passage, if thoroughly explored, would be found to run from the river Irwell, near Water Street to another point close to the river near the Cathedral. There is material for much conjecture in the discovery......There is, too, a story of the mysterious disappearance of a man wanted for murder about half a century ago. The story goes that the man was trailed by the police to a house in this very Cumberland Street He was seen to enter it, but never to leave it. If the story is true, possibly the mystery of the man's escape is explained by the existence of this passage. Knowing of it, he would enter it and make his way underground until he arrived at a point beyond the ken of his pursuers.'

The next account by J LINDLEY refers to another stretch of the tunnel further up Deansgate:

'In 1906 I served my time at Thos. Armstrong & Bro. Deansgate as a clock and instrument maker. The premises were number sixty six which is now where the Houldsworth Hall stands. The building occupied by Armstrong had been years ago the old Deanery - that's where Deansgate got its name. There was a sundial and gardens at the back, and some lovely stained glass windows. In the cellars, which had been wine cellars, was a small door which led to a tunnel. You went down ten or twelve stone steps and then turned left to go towards Wagstaffe's piano shop. I have been along it for quite a distance. I think this would be the one that went to Kendals. I presume it went to the Cathedral. The Deanery was pulled down about 1916, and Armstrong removed to 76 Deansgate.' (JH)

94

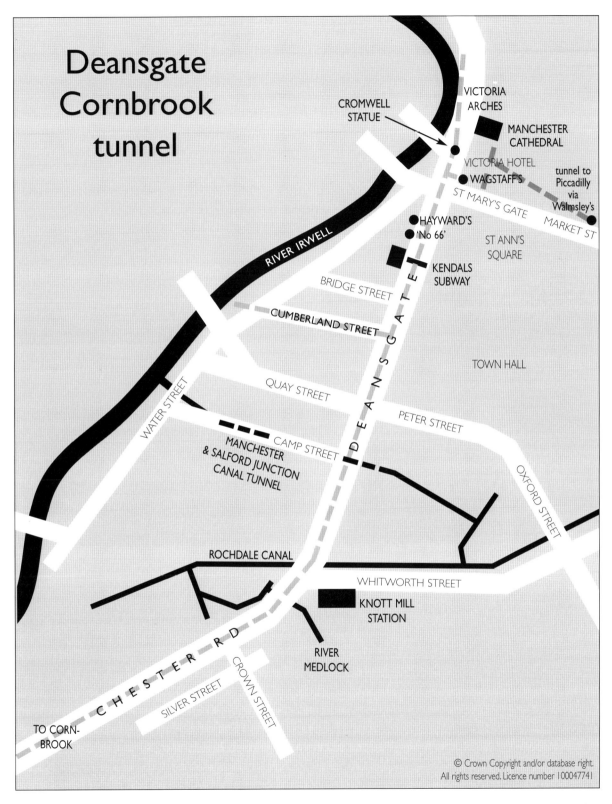

Deansgate
Cornbrook
tunnel

CROMWELL STATUE

VICTORIA ARCHES

MANCHESTER CATHEDRAL

VICTORIA HOTEL

WAGSTAFF'S

tunnel to Piccadilly via Walmsley's

ST MARY'S GATE

MARKET ST

HAYWARD'S

'No 66'

ST ANN'S SQUARE

RIVER IRWELL

KENDALS SUBWAY

BRIDGE STREET

CUMBERLAND STREET

DEANSGATE

TOWN HALL

QUAY STREET

WATER STREET

PETER STREET

CAMP STREET

OXFORD STREET

MANCHESTER & SALFORD JUNCTION CANAL TUNNEL

ROCHDALE CANAL

WHITWORTH STREET

KNOTT MILL STATION

RIVER MEDLOCK

CHESTER RD

CROWN STREET

SILVER STREET

TO CORN-BROOK

BERNARD WEBSTER was an employee at the City Engineers Department and in an interview, he confirms the existence of a tunnel between Kendals and towards the cathedral:

'Wagstaff's Piano Shop was on the corner of Deansgate and St Mary's Gate in the Victoria Hotel Building. Down two flights of stairs there was a tunnel filled with pianos and organs. I went into the tunnel and was told at one point we were under subway level at Kendals.' (JH)

In September 1973 there were reports of a building worker missing in a tunnel under the old Wagstaff's premises during th construction of a new building. (JH)

Wagstaff's was in the block belonging to the Victoria Hotel. The sign can just be seen in the photograph on page 92.

In the 1938 the business at 1-3 St Mary's Gate was listed as Albert Wagstaff Ltd, pianoforte, gramophone, radio, band instruments and organ dealers, concert and ticket bookings office.

EDGAR BRIGGS had nearly fifty years experience with the GPO as a telecommunications engineer, and then as a planning and estimating engineer. In 1974 he was featured in the *Bury Times* because, at the age of 72, he wrote to his local MP, explaining how the cost of the proposed Picc-Vic line could be reduced by using the centuries old tunnel under Deansgate. He claimed the tunnel ran from the Cathedral to just short of Knott Mill. (JH)

To take the trouble to write to his MP suggests that Briggs was fully convinced of the tunnel's existence. Although he was not named, Briggs was more than likely, the man who was interviewed for the Radio Manchester's 'Manchester Underground' series in 1975, and who was certain of a tunnel under Deansgate, running from Hunts Bank to Knott Mill. He had worked for the GPO, and during the last world war he was involved in first aid, which took him to various underground shelters in the City. He knew that a tunnel ran in front of the Cathedral through to St John's Street - the latter section of which he had been down.

He described the tunnel as large enough for a single-decker bus to pass through, lined, and about 70 feet below ground. He thought the entrances near Knott Mill and the Cathedral were tiled. Although he knew of the Manchester and Salford Junction Canal near St John's Street, he had not been down there and was convinced that the two tunnels were entirely separate. [1]

GORDON HAYWARD owner of the glass shop on Deansgate, opposite the Barton Arcade, said in an interview that there was a warehouse passage below the building which ran along Deansgate from Blackfriars to Parsonage. When the lease expired, the business closed, but later inspections of the cellars have not located the entrance to the passage. (JH)

In around 1949 KEITH HAMNETT was an apprentice working on the preparation of the leadwork for the roof of Manchester Cathedral, which was being restored following damage sustained during the war. In an interview for the Manchester Cathedral Archives he remembered:

> '..we stored our lead in the crypt, which was at the opposite
> end to the altar, and it was through a little door which went
> down below into the crypt into the corridors, and the corridors
> led through to the toilets which were then between the
> Cathedral and Exchange Station on an island...In the toilets
> were two doors, one to the left and one to the right. Through
> these doors was 'old Deansgate' which is still there today
> I believe, and it went right up under Deansgate to the end
> at Knott Mill. As far as I know it is still there today. During the
> War it was used for storing tins of corned beef and beans.'

Construction began on Kendals subway in 1921, following the passing of a parliamentary act the previous year, to link its buildings on either side of Deansgate. The subway was open by 4 July of that year, when it was mentioned in an advertisement for their 'Summer Sale of High-Grade Furniture'. The building now occupied by Waterstones, was sold by Kendals and closed in 1981, which also brought the closure of the subway. Part of the subway can still be seen in Kendals. There is also a service tunnel linking the store with a rear warehouse.

The 'crypt' referred to, would have been the cellars. Keith could not recall how he knew about the tunnel under Deansgate when I interviewed him in 2006. I note that there is also a suggestion that the tunnel may have been put to use as a storage area during the Second World War. It would seem that the tunnel was already known to the Civil Defence authorities, although it was never mentioned or considered as a shelter in official documents.

This mysterious route running under the centre of the city is not marked on any maps, nor is it mentioned in any publications or documents. Why was it built, and who built it? It has also been referred to as 'the Roman tunnel'. Perhaps this is because Deansgate was a Roman road, and wide enough to allow four centurions to march side by side. There is no evidence to support such ancient origins.

The Cathedral - does it link with the Deansgate tunnel?

Edgar Briggs calculated the tunnel to be around 70 feet below. This would indicate that it would be well beneath the line of the Manchester and Salford Junction Canal which opened in 1839 and went to a depth of around 37 feet at this point. This is confirmed by Bernard Webster's account which described the tunnel as being accessed down two flights of steps, and 'under subway level at Kendals'.

Both Briggs' and the newspaper description of tiles and brick arches indicate something more substantial than an industrial working. It was a route known to other people - Chris Hill, a member of Altrincham History Society, recalls his father telling him of the tunnel beneath the length of Deansgate. He was told it was a Victorian access route to businesses in the area. William Connell claimed he walked along it, (see later chapter on Connell) and that there was an iron gate at the Cornbrook end where it came on to the side of the Bridgewater Canal.

Connell's story is endorsed by FRED S SEVILLE, a manufacturers' agent who was born in Old Trafford and lived there until his early twenties. He remembered that during excavation, in the 1930s, for the railway tunnel under Chester Road at Trafford Bar, workers

The lodge to trafford Park was moved to its present position outside Gorse Hill Park .

came across a tunnel that was believed to run under Deansgate. The tunnel went from Trafford Hall Lodge through to the cathedral. Fred had a school friend who lived at the lodge which was on the left hand side of Chester road close to Trafford Bar. Within the lodge there was a locked door which led to a shaft with a rope ladder down to the tunnel. Fred later moved to Northern Ireland but in the 1970s, when he passed the lodge where the Henshall family had lived he found it had become a used car saleroom. 1975 (JH)

In 1979 MR A TYLER recalls a childhood incident in which he and his friends seem to have come across the same southern section of the tunnel. He grew up in Hulme and lived in Crown Street (where the Securicor offices are today). Nearby on Silver Street, was a row of houses with basements where he was looked after while his mother worked at the local jam-making factory. It was around here that he found a door open that had previously been padlocked. He and some friends went into a passage and travelled through the darkness until they were frightened by a loud sound above. They had arrived under Whitworth Street and they were found by the police. They later heard that the passage led to Kendals. In about 1932 a Salford firm of builders, Waterfield and Sons, modernising Kendal's basement came across this passage and found it went to the cathedral. Part of the passage went into the toilets and air raid shelter at the end of Victoria Street. (JH)

'They had arrived under Whitworth Street and they were found by the police.'

There are a number of clues about the age of the Deansgate tunnel. It is clear from the newspaper article of 1911 that it was already a 'forgotten' tunnel. At least one local knew of it from fifty years previously and speculated that there were further sections, but it was clearly something new to the newspaper reporter. If Manchester Corporation officials knew of the tunnel they did not respond to the article. It would seem that the existence of the tunnel generally ceased to be known from at least the 1860s. An experienced builder is quoted in the article, stating that the passage could be 'between two and three hundred years old'. How accurate his observation was, is open to speculation.

The same City News article also made suggestions that the tunnel branched off to the River Irwell close to Water Street, and also by the cathedral. Another account says it opens out by the Bridgewater Canal near the Trafford swing bridge. This would also lend weight to the theory that the tunnel is not Roman in origin, but more likely to be a large redundant Victorian sewer. Council officers do not necessarily make public all that lies below the city, but it would seem that a substantial underground route, much further down than the drains, does exist beneath Deansgate. Norman Savory's first-hand description (see opposite page) confirms that the routes under Deansgate and in other parts of the city were brick built and were clearly constructed to be more than just a foot passageway. Haywards and Wagstaffs used the tunnel or adjoining sections as storage space, and Briggs' memories of the tunnel from the 1940s were that it was of a sufficient scale and construction for use in an underground rail system.

The tunnel does not seem to have come under consideration in the last world war to be used as an air-raid shelter, but perhaps, during that period, it had been a secure storage area. Other evidence, presented later in the book will point to the Deansgate tunnel being part of a network which stretched far beyond the boundary of Manchester.

Below Manchester during the Blitz years

NORMAN SAVORY grew up in Salford during the Blitz years, and he has described how he and his friends explored the underground routes beneath Manchester. These are places known to very few people, and Norman, prior to our conversation, had not personally come across anyone who knew about them. He had first-hand experience of tunnels which took them under some of the city's most famous thoroughfares and although they did not take too much notice of their surroundings, they would spend many hours down below, sometimes the whole day.

It was in around 1943, when Norman was ten, that he and his three friends began their underground explorations. During the war-time the schools were closed and they had lots of time on their hands. Parts of the city were in ruins following enemy bombing, and they must have had great fun exploring both above and below ground. Many of the food warehouses behind the cathedral had been hit and their contents spilled onto the streets. Fireman damping down the buildings encouraged Norman's group to take away as much food as they could, which they then used as provisions for their adventures below ground.

Being young, the potential dangers did not occur to them as they made their way through tunnels armed only with a torch. The access point was by an opening in the Victoria Arches below the cathedral. Part of the space was taken by a large air-raid shelter, but beyond were vast caverns and tunnels to other parts of the city. Norman recalls going through a hatch in the underground toilets below the Cromwell statue, which opened into a route they estimated took them as far as below Kendals

store. This tunnel, like all the others, was brick-lined and arched. There were no particular problems with the air, but Norman remembers it was cool, smelt musty, and there were signs of dampness including the sound of dripping water. They decided they had gone far enough by then and made their way back. From what he was able to make out, the tunnel was about nine feet high and wide. There was some light from what he thought were manholes. He did not know how far the tunnel went, but guessed it led at least as far as the Liverpool Road area, where his father was born.

Other routes from Victoria arches took them into the centre of town. They had been below Cannon Street, Cross Street and Corporation Street, and on another occasion, as Norman memorably describes it 'they popped up in Shude Hill'. There were metal ladders leading up to the surface, which they climbed. They managed to force up the man-hole cover and looked around. It was a busy market day and no-one noticed them and then they climbed back down the twenty or so steps and retraced their route.

Norman had heard that there was a tunnel route up Great Ducie Street under the old Assize Courts going on towards Bury New Road, but had not personally explored it. He also remembered exploring tunnels in a brick works near Queen's Road and a sandy area at Kersal Moor. Norman's account of the Manchester tunnels confirms the recollections of others featured in this book. He and his friends explored each tunnel on two occasions and then their attentions turned to a completely different activity, this time above ground, climbing trees in Prestwich Clough.[2]

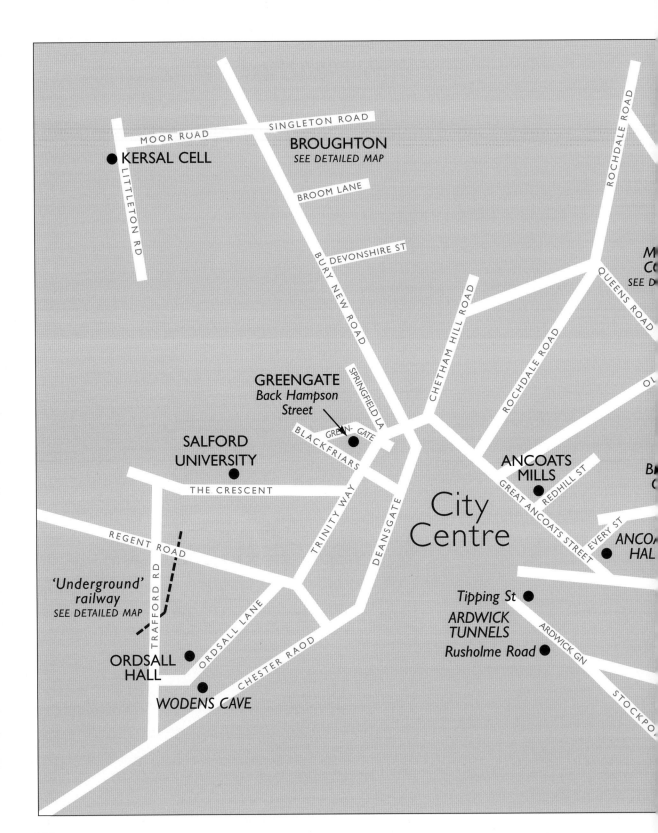

SINGLETON ROAD

MOOR ROAD

● KERSAL CELL

BROUGHTON
SEE DETAILED MAP

BROOM LANE

LITTLETON RD

BURY NEW ROAD

DEVONSHIRE ST

ROCHDALE ROAD

M...
C...
SEE D...

QUEENS ROAD

CHETHAM HILL ROAD

GREENGATE
*Back Hampson
Street*

SPRINGFIELD LA

GREEN- GATE

BLACKFRIARS

SALFORD
UNIVERSITY
●

ROCHDALE ROAD

ANCOATS
MILLS
●

REDHILL ST

B...
C...

THE CRESCENT

TRINITY WAY

DEANSGATE

GREAT ANCOATS STREET

EVERY ST

ANCO...
HAL...
●

City
Centre

REGENT ROAD

TRAFFORD RD

'Underground'
railway
SEE DETAILED MAP

ORDSALL LANE

Tipping St ●

ARDWICK
TUNNELS
Rusholme Road ●

ARDWICK GN

ORDSALL
HALL
●

CHESTER RAOD

WODENS CAVE
●

STOCKPO...

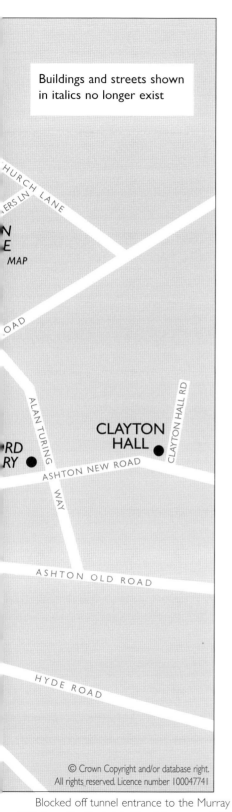

Buildings and streets shown
in italics no longer exist

HURCH LANE

ERS LN

*N
E*

MAP

OAD

ALAN TURING WAY

CLAYTON
HALL

CLAYTON HALL RD

*RD
RY*

ASHTON NEW ROAD

ASHTON OLD ROAD

HYDE ROAD

Blocked off tunnel entrance to the Murray
Mills from the Rochdale Canal (see page 105)

Around Manchester
and parts of Salford

Ancoats Hall

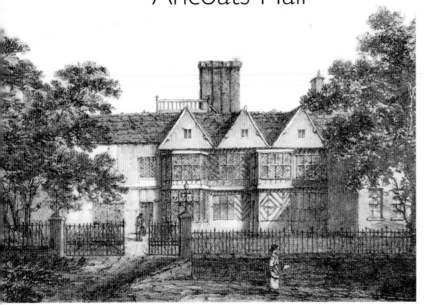

Ancoats Hall stood on the site bounded by Great Ancoats Street, Every Street and Palmerston Street. From 1886 it was known as the Art museum, visited by many local schools, and later also housed the University Settlement, a voluntary organisation dedicated to working alongside the community. The Hall had deep Elizabethan cellars, and there are several accounts of tunnels in the vicinity.

'As a boy I attended Birley Street School in Beswick. We were taken frequently to the Horsfall Museum which then stood on the corner of Every Street and Great Ancoats Street. We believed that a tunnel ran from the Museum to the Cathedral though the curator was reluctant to confirm this was so. He did say he thought it had caved in a few yards from the house and the entrance had been bricked up. However the man I remember as caretaker was far more generous with information. He told me there was a tunnel but it did not go to the Cathedral. His story was that it connected with a larger tunnel which ran from Ardwick Green to a large cavern which existed between the Cathedral main door and the River Irwell.'
C HARRISON 1974 (JH)

Owen Murray of Ardwick knew of a tunnel here. It was under a double cellar and he found it when he fell down into it. He also knew of a tunnel under Pin Mill Brow - possibly on the same route. The entrance was flagged and sealed up (JH)

Ken Naylor remembered the Art Museum when he delivered newspapers to the University Settlement based there. He went to Every Street School around the age of seven. His aunt managed the Railway Inn and lived at Ancoats Hall. Below the inn was a large coal cellar with smaller cellars leading off. There is another reference to a tunnel in the SE corner of the cellar at the Horsfall Inn. There were two long passages, and one of them went about 400 yards under the road in the direction of Pin Mill Brow. He was 15 when he explored the tunnel which was about 6 feet high and at least 6 feet wide - he could not touch the sides with his outstretched arms in the dark. The tunnel had a slight curve and his aunt told him it went into the centre of Manchester, and in the other direction to Clayton.

There was a tunnel below All Soul's Church, in Every Street, running horizontally with it. This was discovered in the old graveyard after excavation began for flats on the site. There were gates large enough for a car to pass through. The tunnel was about 10 feet down and travelled under Every Street towards the Don Cinema. (JH)

The Manchester Evening News reported twenty feet deep subsidence on Every Street in 1958 which revealed old brickwork below.

William Connell had a graphic description of going in the tunnel under the Hall (See page 139).

In 1961 a huge hole appeared on Chancellor Lane, Ardwick, south of the Ancoats Hall site, following subsidence. The 30 feet deep and 20 feet wide crater was inspected, and both the Electricity and North Western Gas Boards declared that there was no danger to the public and supplies were unaffected.

Ancoats Mills

The 1848 Ordnance Survey plans reveal tunnels running under Bengal Street between the Murray Mills on Redhill Street, then known as Union Street. One tunnel linked a canal basin in the centre of the Old and New Mills to the Rochdale Canal, bringing in coal and raw cotton. The tunnel would have been too small for the normal canal boats and so smaller craft were used. Two other smaller passages are thought to have been used for taking coal between the two sites. Later insurance plans of 1927 indicate that there were four tunnels beneath Bengal Street.

The mills were constructed between 1798 and 1806, and are the world's oldest surviving steam-powered urban cotton mills. Thirteen men, women and children worked here in what was regarded at the time of building as an industrial marvel. The mills continued to be used for cotton spinning until the late 1950s, and then for other textile use.

In 1891 the basin was marked on maps as a 'reservoir' and by 1902 it had been filled in. It has been re-excavated during redevelopment work which began in 2004. The tunnel to the basin was possibly used to bring water to the steam plant until the 1950s.

Ardwick -Tipping street

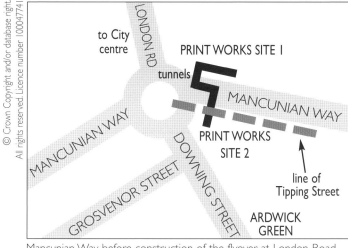

Mancunian Way before construction of the flyover at London Road.

During work for the Mancunian Way flyover at London Road and Downing Street, a canal tunnel network was found in April 1991 going under Tipping Street (originally Medlock Street). This is believed to be a source of the water supply between the two sites of Ardwick Print works, as previously reported in 1905:

During the process of sinking a shaft for the new sewerage scheme in Manchester, at a depth of sixteen to eighteen feet below the street, the workmen came across what appeared to be the brick arch of an old sewer. When broken through there appeared, at a further depth of ten feet, a reservoir of dark coloured, though clear water, ten feet deep. Several people ventured in a boat on this underground water, and travelled three hundred yards in one direction and one hundred in the opposite direction. The reservoir had been hewn from the red sandstone rock, and although the air was fairly pure there was no apparent inlet or outlet.

The shaft spoken of was, according to my informant, in Tipping Street, near to Downing Street, and the reservoir ran from the direction of Grosvenor Street towards Hoyle's printworks, fully twenty feet below the bed of the Medlock.
SANDFOLD. MANCHESTER CITY NEWS 1905

A large cavern was accidentally discovered here in 1936, when a garage was under construction at the corner of Downing Street and Tipping Street. A labourer slipped on a plank and his barrow disappeared into a watery hole.

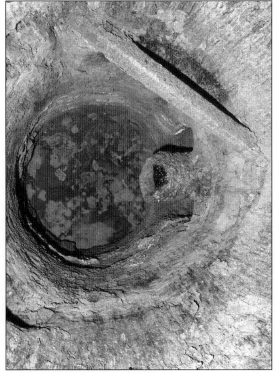

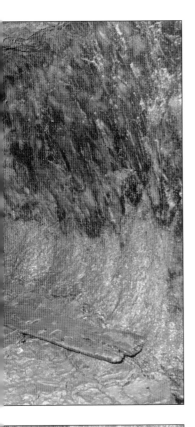

Ardwick - Rusholme Road

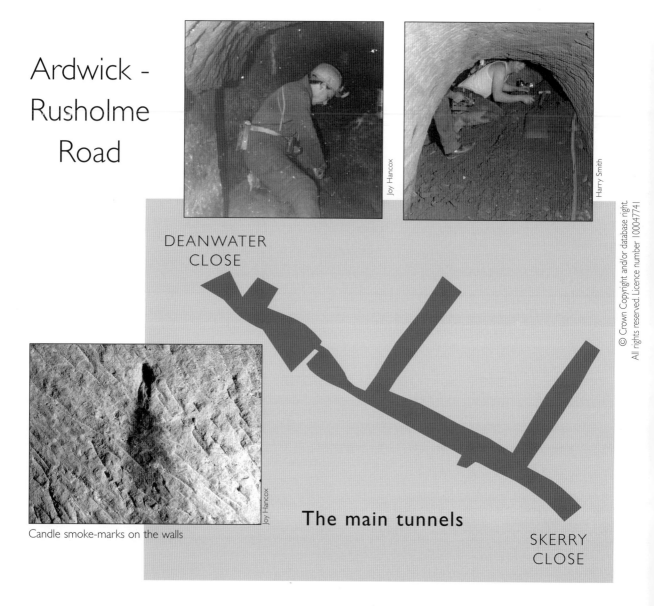

Joy Hancox

Harry Smith

DEANWATER CLOSE

The main tunnels

SKERRY CLOSE

Candle smoke-marks on the walls

Joy Hancox

The Ministry of Housing approved the clearance of 54 acres in the Rusholme Road area of Ardwick in 1961. A thousand homes were to be demolished to make way for 1500 new dwellings. During routine excavation in 1964, an extensive set of shafts and tunnels was found close to Ardwick Green. Workmen found a 6 feet wide shaft cut into solid sandstone which led down to a 24 feet high, 45 feet long and 15 feet wide chamber with an arched roof. At 4 feet intervals, ledges had been cut into the stone for either candles or miner's lamps. Above them are the black markings from the smoke. Marks of the miners' picks are to be seen on the walls. Seventeen shafts and tunnels were discovered in the soft red sandstone, with several smaller side chambers. The shafts had been filled with rubbish, rubble and bits of pottery dating back to the early 1800s.

Corporation workmen removed water and rubble from the tunnel and the system remained dry. This large working had been carefully constructed, possibly using miner's picks. No abandoned tools were found. The new housing was not built directly over the tunnel; its route is underneath gardens and open spaces.

'The access to the chamber appeared as a depression in the bottom of a sewer trench which fell away, revealing a 5ft diameter circular shaft in the soft red sandstone with a chamber off one side of it. On exploration, the chamber was very uniformly shaped and tooled, and 30ft below ground. At first the chamber contained approximately 9ft of water, but after the loose filling material was removed the water percolated away through the sandstone. In the sides of the chamber are a number of recesses, each of which has a soot mark above it, indicating that at one time the chamber was well lit, presumably by wicks in tallow, some remains of the tallow were found in the pockets.

In addition to the chamber a number of circular shafts were also found, each of which was connected by a system of tunnels approximately 3ft by 2ft wide. The finish on the sandstone was not quite as even as these as on the chamber, but the roof shape was very similar.

The loose filling material which was found in the tunnels and chamber contained fragments of pottery which was dated late 18th century. The first system of sewers in this area was constructed between 1800 and 1840 and presumably the tunnel and chamber were loosely filled in at that time'.

City Engineers' house magazine, THE HIGHWAYMAN 1967 (JH)

Joy Hancox

Ken Howarth

Ken Howarth

There are a number of theories regarding the reason for this 'mysterious labyrinth', including as a reservoir for a planned ship canal which would come through south Manchester in 1825, a quarry, a continuation of the Bridgewater Canal, or to supply water. Engineers found wells at a deeper level which were constructed differently, and there is speculation that the tunnels were an army exercise. This could have been to practice at tunnelling prior to strengthening the defences of the Rock of Gibraltar, which was confirmed as British territory in a 1783 Treaty. This theory would explain why tunnels and shafts had been built so close together, and why they were basically dry. One of the shafts had a large slab over it, which in turn was covered by a sewer put in during house building in about 1825. An earlier plan of 1810 indicates a building project here. By 1845 most of the area was covered in housing developments, although it may be significant that there was a remaining stoneyard adjoining the houses. Was stone from the mine sold here? This site is not be confused with the nearby fire-clay working beneath Ashton New Road, which was abandoned in 1905.

Bradford Colliery

Coal has been excavated from the Bradford district since at least the sixteenth century. It was an important supplier, along with the pits at Worsley, Moston and Clayton, to Manchester's cotton mills and factories with the coming of the Industrial Revolution. In 1740 ten miners were employed on the shallow workings, but by 1845 the mining was much deeper, with coal being wound up through a shaft. A brickworks was built on the site after deeper workings revealed seams of fireclay which was used in the making of firebricks for lining furnaces.

The first modern shaft was sunk in 1854 and was thought to be the second deepest in the British coalfields. In 1896 404 underground and 125 surface workers were employed there.

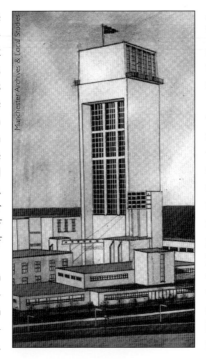

Manchester Archives & Local Studies

A second shaft was completed in 1906. Work started in 1948 to make the colliery Britain's first 'super-pit', and the design of the site was described as resembling a 'holiday camp'. By 1953 production had increased and the reconstruction, estimated at three million pounds, was half-way to completion. In 1958 Ashton Moss Colliery was merged with Bradford, which helped to boost production figures. By 1962, three teams of 144 miners produced 11,500 tons, compared with 8,500 tons the previous year - the best-ever results from one coal face in a week. Record figures were achieved at the West Roger coal face, the longest in the country, by combining the number three and four faces.

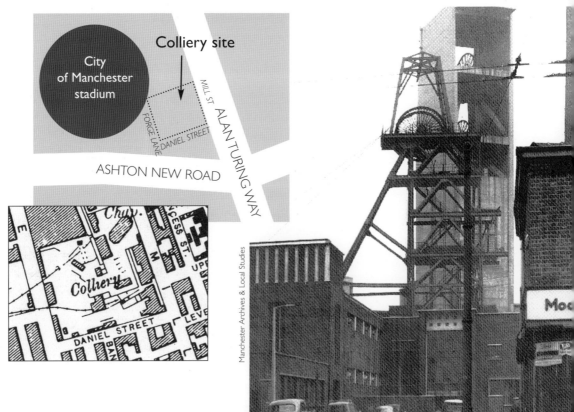

Manchester Archives & Local Studies

CITY PIT TO YIELD 4,000 TONS A DAY

'The first pit to be approved by the National Coal Board for complete conversion to horizon mining technique will produce 4,600 tons of coal a day for at least 60 years from underneath the central city area of Manchester.

It is the Bradford Pit, where all existing surface buildings will be razed to the ground and an area of adjoining private property demolished. In their place will rise a 245 ft tower - rivalled for height by only Manchester Town Hall - and an assembly of buildings resembling a holiday camp rather than a working colliery. Bradford Colliery, with deep and steeply inclined coal seams, produces 800 tons a day on one shift with 800 men. The plan is to produce 4,000 tons a day with fewer than 2,000 men, working two shifts and covering a wider underground area.

Thus about a ton a manshift overall is planned to become two tons. This will be done by:
1 - Transfers of miners from less productive pits to Bradford.
2 - Adoption of horizon mining - the driving of two horizontal tunnel systems, one below the other, to intersect the dipping coal seams, and shifting the coal by small vertical shafts to the level tunnelling where electric locomotives will haul trains of three-ton mine cars to pit bottom. Coal between the first two tunnels will last 20 years.
3 - Skip-winding in nine ton skips to the surface, automatic surface handling of the coal, and even mechanical coal bagging.

An outstanding feature will be the construction of a 450yd long, 50ft deep tunnel and shaft system from the colliery to the neighbouring Stuart Street Power Station for direct conveyor belt delivery of 30 per cent of the colliery's output. The power station will reciprocate by powering the colliery. Manchester Corporation will share the cost of this part of the colliery extension between Forge Lane and Mill Street.'

DAILY DISPATCH 1948

There were two seams going towards Newton Heath and Moston, and a further two in the direction of Holt Town and Ancoats. Both shafts were 900 yds (823m) deep.

No 1 shaft (downcast) carried fresh air down and had a 'cage' for the movement of miners and supplies. One miner recalls that the descent by the steam winder could be 'heart-stoppingly fast' in the 1950s. No 2 shaft removed the stale air and brought up the coal in 2 12-ton skips.

The successful output figures and further expansion plans were overshadowed by concerns about damage to property due to mining subsidence.

Manchester Archives & Local Studies

By August 1962 there were press reports that the colliery had caused over a million pounds' worth of damage to houses, factories, and underground water, electricity, and gas services. It was said to be threatening further major industrial plants in the city. Claims for compensation had been lodged with the National Coal Board, but under the 1957 Act compensation was not payable for the interruption of business. The damage was mainly in the Bradford Collyhurst areas of the city, where the Bradford Road gasholder had tilted and was

and the board hoped to help out the businesses and people affected. Homes in the Princess Street and New Street area had cracked and developed bulging walls, and yet the Coal Board were planning to start a new 600-yard shaft below land scheduled for new houses. There were even cracked water mains to be found in New Street, and thirty seven people had be evacuated from flats in Collyhurst. Compensation was offered by the Coal Board who feared that the outcome of the subsidence would be the loss of 1700 mining jobs.

1966

CHEETAM HILL RD

BURY NEW ROAD

ROCHDALE RD

QUEENS ROAD

OLDHAM ROAD

Roger Seam

Crambouke Seam

GT ANCOATS ST

ASHTON NEW RD

Piccadilly

ASHTON OLD ROAD

Tunnel link between the Ashton Moss and Bradford pits.

MINI
UNRE
Buildings
walls b

Meetings are between the Coal B local factory owner and householders ting, following damage to proper mining subsidence Householders in street – New - st complaining of bulging walls, w t,ory has been pu or the present

restricted to half the normal capacity. Municipal buildings, including a fire station, and a swimming pool, were sinking, and cracks had appeared in homes causing many to be demolished. The brick bed of a river, which took the water through the district, had crumbled and distorted. Local factories had been seriously damaged and machinery was regularly reset to adjust for the shifting foundations. Fractures to water mains and sewers, and subsiding roads and footpaths were also major problems.

The problems had begun when the National Coal Board began to modernise the pit, which was employing around 1,700 miners. The Coal Board admitted that surface damage would occur wherever coal was worked. This was to be expected in an industrial area,

One thousand homes were planned for Collyhurst, which would mean sacrificing one of the coal industry's greatest assets.

Maps drawn in 1965 indicate that the Roger Seam workings extended west close to Great Ancoats Street, when there were 1600 men working at the pit. Significantly it was also the year when Manchester Corporation gained Government approval to control any further expansion of coal mining under the city.

In 1966 the Coal Board requested authority to extend mining operations in Manchester in order to increase profits. A public enquiry was held in the city where the Board argued that if the mine was closed

£10 million of coal would be lost and 1600 men would lose their jobs.

Then in 1968 it was announced that Bradford Colliery would close in the September of that year. Ultimately it was not the subsidence but other problems which caused its downfall

The pit had been profitable from 1963 to 1966, but in spite of predictions of increasing profits, the following financial year it lost one million pounds. The decline continued in 1968 and the Board decided they could not continue to run the loss-making pit. They noted in a statement that until that time 'the only danger to the pit was the possibility that Manchester Corporation would halt the extension of mining operations because of subsidence.' Reasons given for the reversal of fortune were geological faults, an underground fire, and the 'failure to keep expensive coal-cutting machinery running for long enough each shift'.

In the year of its closure, the output was 538,808 tons of coal, and there had been plans for more seams under Ancoats, Cheetham and Collyhurst. It is claimed that there were around 300,000 tons of coal reserves remaining at Bradford. The miners voted to accept the closure, accepting that there was no point in prolonging the life of the ailing pit, following the adverse reports.

One of the miners remembered 'walking underground from the old Ashton Moss colliery, prior to its demolition and capping, to Bradford colliery and at a later date walking underground to almost under the CIS building by Victoria Station in central Manchester. The western area was the deepest in the UK at the time, very hot and wet.'

The winding gear on the two shafts was demolished

Demolition of the winding gear

in 1973. Machinery considered not worth salvaging was buried on the two acre site. Concrete stoppers were inserted into the mouths of the horizontal tunnels which led off from the two vertical pit shafts. Reenforced concrete plugs 30 feet in diameter and 6 feet thick were placed 120 feet beneath the surface to seal off the shafts which were then filled to ground level. They were then thought to be absolutely safe and free from subsidence.

The only inhabitants to remain below were the mice who must have first got into the mine via the timbers taken down to strengthen the pit-shaft. Others would have followed in the tubs moving up and down the shafts. The mice lived on scraps from the miners' snap tins and sometimes, when the pit closed for annual holidays, miners left behind loaves of stale bread for them.

The old colliery entrance is on the site of Manchester City's Eastlands Stadium and many ex-miners have been campaigning for a memorial for the men who died at the pit.

Occasionally coal seams were found under the Manchester streets. In 1933 a 3 feet thick seam was found at the corner of Oldham Road and Nelson Street, Miles Platting, 70 feet below during sewer excavations. The coal was brought up in skips and left by the roadside. Eager locals, some of whom would have been too poor to afford coal, took it away before the police arrived to cordon off the area. A seam fifty feet below was discovered in Collyhurst by workmen in 1938.

Manchester Archives & Local Studies

90 degrees ... a mile below ... to mine the coal

The giant reinforced cage bounced gently on the end of 2800 feet of steel cable, and somebody mentioned casually that we were almost three-quarters of a mile underground. I shivered, and looked through the barred door of the cage - into the dimly lit main tunnel at the foot of Number One Shaft, Bradford Colliery.

Bradford, a mere fourpenny ride from Piccadilly, Manchester, is one of the larger collieries in this country, employing almost one and a half thousand men and pouring out half a million tons of coal a year.

My guides on the journey to the coal face were the colliery Safety Officer, Tom Jones, and the Area Safety Officer, Charles Clay, and we set off from the shaft to walk to where the colliers were excavating the 6 feet thick high-quality Roger Seam - one of the largest and cleanest struck at the colliery since the shafts were sunk in the1850s.

The ventilation system for the 46 miles of tunnel is controlled by steel doors set in the rock, which maintain a steady flow of air throughout, and these had to be negotiated at intervals. These underground 'roadways' are known in the collieries as 'levels' but I quickly found that they are anything but level!

As we walked away from the shaft bottom, the roof lights ended, and we relied on the battery lamps clipped on to our composite helmets.

Everywhere was coated in a thick layer of stone dust, and I was thankful for the boiler-suit and iron soled boots which the mine officials insist visitors wear.

I asked Mr Clay if the dust is harmful to the lungs - and received the surprising answer that most of the dust has been put there by the colliers. It is 'stone dust,' and acts as a fire preventive. It is not harmful in any way.

As the incline of the 'level' increased, the going became decidedly harder and we perspired freely. It was then that I learnt that the deeper you go, it becomes hotter, and hotter and hotter. And the men working the deepest coal face at Bradford hew and shovel continually in a temperature of 90 degrees F, while the rocks themselves are 106 degrees before they are cooled down by the life-giving air, pumped down at 360,000 cubic feet every minute. This is at a depth of about one mile, vertically, from the surface.

As Safety Officer, Mr Jones carries out a daily inspection, and there is a continual flow of reports on the safety measures and conditions at coal level, day and night from a team of 40 deputies.

The tunnel became steeper and the roof lowered, our progress slowed down, and Mr Clay assured me that the tunnel had been built 10 feet high and 14 feet wide. 'The floor has risen quite quickly here. he said.'And as you can see, the roof is gradually forcing the supports down.'

I looked up, and saw that what had once been firm rounded bastions had been reduced to tangled, twisted metal skeletons that cast weird shadows in the light of our lamps.

Life below ground is one long fight against the pressure of the earth above, at the sides, and below, and nothing can be left to chance. As rock and coal is removed, stout wooden props shore up the roof. Picking our way over the coal truck lines on the tunnel floor, we forced back yet another steel door - it closed with a muffled clang that echoed down the black tunnel - and I could see lights bobbing and weaving in the distance ... the coal face, and one of the main objects of our journey.

Drawing near to the workings, I could hear the harsh chatter of pneumatic drills, biting deep into the rock walls and the deafening whine of steel against unyielding shale.

The scene, to anyone ignorant of mining, like myself, was almost chaotic. Through the murky pall of dust which swirled everywhere, my lamp lit up piles of pit props and rubble; and coal-dust blackened colliers, most of them stripped to the waist, as they strained and sweated, shovelling coal on to a form of metal conveyor belt. Somewhere out of sight in the inky blackness, the only

Manchester Archives & Local Studies

evidence of their presence, a cone of light from their lamps, which cleft the dark as they moved, and the sharp clang of a pick-axe.

'Co-operation,' said Mr Jones, 'is the only way to solve problems at the coal-face.' And he pointed to where the manager of the mine himself, Mr H Taylor, a foreman and several colliers were thrashing out a tricky problem of roof supports - each man having his say, regardless of his position on the surface.

The seams at Bradford often occur at inclines of 1 in 2, due to the Pennine uplift, and as we moved along the coal face, it dipped sharply until we had to slither along on our steel-capped boots, holding on to the wooden supports to stop us from falling. To the left of the level, a metal conveyor - in sections - was carrying coal downwards to one of the main belts in the larger level below. In a mine, all belts lead to the tippler, where the coal is taken away for sorting.

We left the coal face a little farther down and dropped into one of the main - or trunk tunnels - in the colliery. High, and quite well lit by electric lamps on the ceiling, it was one of the tunnels along which the underground trains tow 100-ton loads of coal to the tippler.

Although I didn't see a load in progress, I had a ride on one of the 90 horse power, battery-driven engines. And it's quite an experience, I can assure you, to travel on a swaying locomotive along a murky tunnel - a mile underground.

Nearing the tippler, and the bottom of the lift-shaft, we encountered more and more people - officials on routine inspections, colliers going 'on shift' - and the high tunnels, which joined our level, I found to be underground loco sheds, where the engines are stored and serviced, and their batteries charged.

But one of the highlights of the tour was yet to come. It was the tippler itself, which actually turns the huge steel trucks over, in a complete circle to empty the coal down into the preparation section.

Our ascent from the shaft bottom, passing the point where we had alighted on the way down, was not as spectacular as the descent, when the cage plummets down at about 20 miles an hour in mid-shaft. A 1700 hp winding engine ensures a smooth lift.

● *From an article by an un-named reporter in the Manchester & Suburban News 18 August 1960*

Clayton Hall

There are 'stories' of a tunnel connecting the Art Museum, Every Street, Ancoats, with Clayton Hall, the Sir Humphrey Chetham pub and Manchester Cathedral but no evidence has been produced. Excavations to lay a sewer in the grounds in 1973, uncovered a well-preserved wooden drain thought to be over two hundred years old. It seemed to run from the house towards the moat but there was uncertainty about whether it was a drain from the moat or if it was used as a sewer.

Coal Board records indicate an old seam directly under the hall and close to the surface.(JH)

Collyhurst

A 1882 newspaper letter describes a passage in the red sandstone quarries off Collyhurst Road near the junction of Moston Brook with the River Irk. The tunnel ran from Collyhurst Road, towards a spot in the clough, then known locally as the site of an old castle or castellated mansion. A short length of the passage had been cleared, five feet high and three feet wide. It is well constructed but there has been a roof fall. Two side galleries were to be seen. This was probably the original Moston Brook culvert.

Moston Brook emerging from beneath the premises of HMB Paints' Riverside works on Collyhurst Road.

Greengate, Salford

King William IV pub

There is an account of a tunnel which could be accessed from a yard in Back Hampson Street, Salford which went as far as Greengate. It was possibly used for storage by a brewery, and thought to pass under the cellar of a public house near the river. On Springfield Lane, near the King William IV pub there was evidence of a 100-feet long road collapse. A lady interviewed by Radio Manchester in 1974 had been down steps under Back Hampson Street to the blocked-off tunnel entrance which was large enough for a small car to pass through. There was no remaining evidence of where it might have ended on the banks of the River Irwell.

There is said to be a tunnel from the cellar of the Old Bull Pub to the Cathedral. My mother saw it when she was six. SEAN MURPHY (JH)

Moston

Moston Cottage

There used to be several old cottages on Potters Lane, also known as Moston Bottoms. A tunnel entrance was found beneath Moston Cottage after local builders Johnny and Ian Roberts fell through weakened floorboards in the front porch in the 1960s. In the space below, thought to be a priest hole, there was straw on the floor, and there were steps which led to a large iron door with a handle.

There were also entrances to the same tunnel from the nearby Crofters House on Moss Brook Road and also from the old paper mill opposite Moston Cottage. In the 1920s Mrs Cleworth's father, Edward Fitzgerald, went with his brother into the tunnel, which they claimed brought them into the centre of Manchester, exiting behind the altar at the Cathedral. Another group in the tunnel turned back in the vicinity of Queens Road. (JH)

Mrs Cleworth's daughter, Hazel, remembers playing in parts of the tunnel when she was little. The section under the cottage was 'damp and smelly' and had a large iron gate. She also knew of airshafts along its route. Brian Maltby who used to work at the Dogs' Home at Crofters Cottage said there was a tunnel in one of the store rooms, which went a few yards under the building, but it had been bricked up.

The Cleworth family believe that the tunnel was a secret route used in times of Catholic persecution. Moston Cottage, a grade two listed building, will be remembered by many as the Moston Brook Animal Sanctuary. A Latin inscription over the front porch confirmed that the cottage was built in 1713 and the mill opposite, the following year.

Moston Cottage

Other people knew of the tunnels in the vicinity: D CAWTHORNE knew of the old cottages on Potters Lane which were said to have a tunnel leading to Manchester Cathedral. (1973 JH). O MURRAY wrote about an old tunnel running under Harpurhey with an ancient water gate. (JH)

There are several problems in accepting the validity of a long tunnel route ending at the cathedral in the 1920s. There are no other accounts of a tunnel from beyond Harpurhey into the city. More importantly, the passage would have the severe engineering difficulty of passing beneath the river Irk, and then find it impossible to enter from beneath the cathedral, whose crypt was sealed in 1865. It is difficult to explain the reasons for the presence of tunnels as seen by Hazel Cleworth and Brian Maltby beneath the two cottages. While they could be routes used in earlier times, there may have been more recent underground workings close to Moston brook. Maps surveyed in 1888 show an explosives store, two dye works and a brick works nearby which would have required drainage and water storage tunnels.

The artist, LS Lowry was a friend of the Cleworths who were the last owners of Moston Cottage. As well as featuring the cottage in three of his works, Lowry also helped to research its history. The owner in 1713 was Samuel Taylor who also owned the wadding mill, described as 'a place of sweated labour', opposite the cottage. A soldier from Bonnie Prince Charlie's retreating army is said to have taken refuge at the cottages, which stood on the site of earlier buildings. In 1996, a compulsory purchase order was served on the owners, and within days of their moving out, vandals had so badly damaged the building that the council had it demolished. It is thought by the Cleworth family that the tunnels were destroyed with the culverting of Moston Brook in 1969.

Ordsall Hall

The hall has been linked with a number of tunnel stories. They usually involve underground routes to Manchester passing under the river Irwell. As this would be a near impossible engineering feat, these can be discounted. Excavations over recent years did not reveal any tunnels but this newspaper article (right) described the interesting find - an underground passage leading from the hall.

The present staff at the hall have no record of any excavations during this period, but during 2007 the exciting discovery was made of a fifteen-feet deep well under the kitchens.

The same correspondent from City News had also checked the report in 1915 of a subterranean passage in Everard Street, Ordsall. The chamber was 22 feet long and 6 feet six inches high and wide, roughly cut into the red sandstone. There was no masonry or remains of any kind, and it lay in a northwest-southeast direction. At the northwest end running northeast was a small tunnel running about three yards into the rock. This was around 2 feet wide and the bottom was 3 feet above the main chamber. The cavern was thought to be either a water storage area or a storage cellar for a house.

> 'There is no doubt that many of our older halls were provided with these secret exits and entrances, though their importance has been much exaggerated. In the case of Ordsall Hall, for instance, the story ran that such a passage began on the eastern side, crossed the river Irwell and terminated in the cellars of Hulme Hall. When Ordsall was restored some dozen years ago, a flag walled passage was discovered which led from a secret chamber in the hall, crossed the lawn, went underneath the moat and terminated abruptly some 20 yards away within an area occupied until the year 1872 by a large outhouse or barn which I well remember before its demolition in that or following year.'
>
> GHR CITY NEWS 1915

The 'Pilgrimage' Tunnels

KERSAL CELL

From the 12th century, Kersal Cell was a small monastic establishment and remained so for four hundred years. During the reign of King John, Crusader Sir Hugo de Burun, at the death of his wife, renounced his title and property to become a hermit here. After the dissolution of the monasteries, four generations of the Kenyon family lived in the reconstructed manor house on the site. The Byrom family were the next owners, including John Byrom who penned the famous carol 'Christians Awake' and is known for his support for the Jacobite cause. He also achieved fame by patenting a method of shorthand.

The house, which had been used as a boarding school for young ladies in the late nineteenth century, was offered for sale by Capt Luttrell Byrom to Salford Council in 1936. The offer was turned down, and fears over the future of building led to a preservation campaign and plans to open it as a museum. Over the following years it was used as a country club and pub. Visitors and members were fascinated by many of its features including a gargoyle in the old refectory which contained a listening device. People in the upper chapel could eavesdrop on conversations by means of a listening tube.

By 1999 the building, which is one of the last remaining examples of sixteenth century domestic architecture in Greater Manchester, had been converted into three homes. Many of its original items had been retained, such as old oak panelling and 16th century plaster-work, which depicts a lion's head and imaginary creatures.

There have been claims of a tunnel running from

Kersal Cell to the vicinity of Manchester Cathedral. There is a story of Roman Catholic followers going on a 'pilgrimage' through a tunnel from Kersal Cell and emerging close to the Lady Chapel at the cathedral, around the late 1870s or early 1880s. An article in the *Manchester Evening News* in 1973 quotes Mrs Winifred Weatherby from Rossendale who recalls her mother telling her about it. The tunnel was said to be high enough to walk through; it had a solid floor, and went towards Bishops Court on Bury New Road. This was the residence of the Bishop of Manchester in Broughton Park. The tunnel walkers knew they had reached this point because they could hear the sound of the horses' hooves on the road above them.

While this may seem difficult to accept, there have been

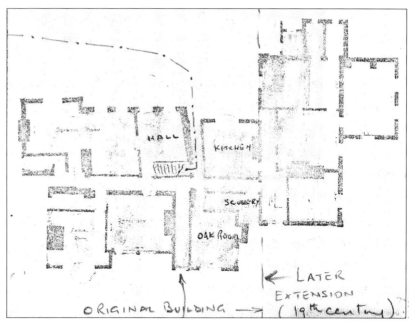

some significant underground finds both at Kersal Cell and along parts of the route. HARRY THOMASSON was shown around Kersal Cell by his father ROWLAND who was a Manchester architect and surveyor (1886-1968), based at 87

Harry Thomasson's sketch plan of the location of the tunnel under Kersal Cell

Staircase at Kersal Cell thought to be the access point to the tunnel

Mosley Street, and who then later joined Manchester Surveyors Department to work on the 1945 City of Manchester Plan. Rowland had done survey work at Kersal Cell and he was assisted by his son there in 1947. Harry recalled being shown reports of the underground passages and said: '(his father).. *showed me a small room which I am almost a hundred per cent certain was under* the staircase in the main hall, and told me that when they had lifted some of the floor stones they had found the entrance to a passage.

It went along under a passage alongside the Hall, out to the rear of the Hall some 20 or so feet and then angled left to the river to come out at a point almost opposite the Cell but a few yards only upstream - possibly to a landing stage, when the river was navigable'.

The passage was brick-lined and dated by Mr Thomasson senior as early to mid 18th century. It was 2 feet wide and 5 feet 6in high. Harry saw some of the tops of the brick walls of the passage outside the building where they had been uncovered. (1972 JH)

An ex fireman also recalled an entrance to a tunnel under the main staircase near the entrance (1974 JH).

CP Hampson wrote in1936 in the Transactions of Lancashire and Cheshire Antiquarian Society:
'Mr Bamber, the occupier of Kersal Cell made the discovery of an underground tunnel running parallel with the house beneath the drive on the north side. It was found after part of the drive collapsed beneath the weight of a heavy lorry delivery of coal. The section was dry and about 6 feet high and wide enough to walk along and seemed of ancient construction. Both ends had been walled up with brick, and looked to go in the direction of the river'.

A local newspaper in 1966 made reference to the road collapse and the discovery of the tunnel some years previously which was thought to be of ancient construction. By this time Kersal Cell was being used as a country club, and the tunnel was reported to be a favourite topic of conversation.

ALAN SHEPHERD knew of the entrance to a tunnel below the staircase. He had been along the passage between Kersal Cell and the hall when he was twelve, when the house had been unoccupied. The passage went to the old stables under a rock outcrop and out towards Oaklands Road. An entrance had been uncovered by the river bank. (1974 JH)

By 2003 Kersal Cell* had been restored but the owner at that time, although aware of the tunnel stories, had not found any evidence.

*Kersal Cell is a private residence

Staircase at Kersal Cell

Joy Hancox

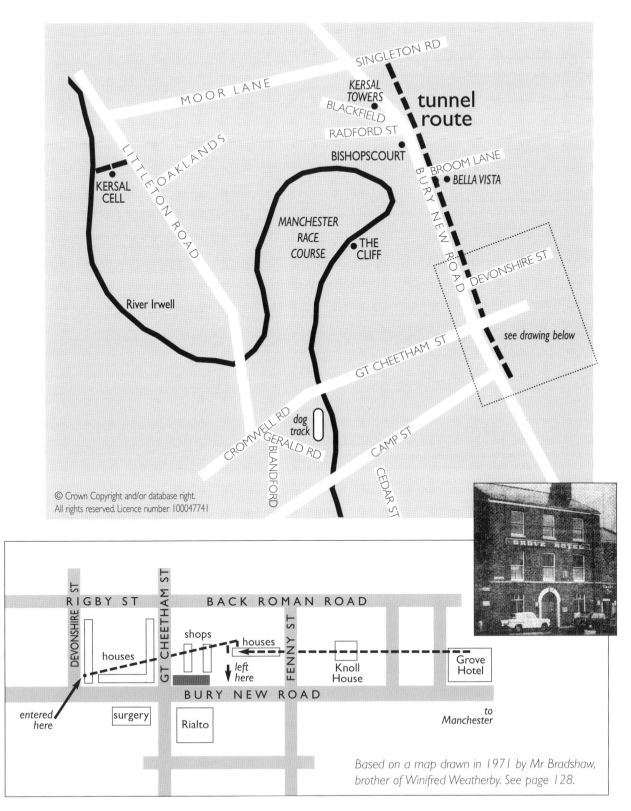

SINGLETON RD

MOOR LANE

KERSAL
TOWERS

BLACKFIELD

RADFORD ST

tunnel route

BISHOPSCOURT

BROOM LANE

BELLA VISTA

LITTLETON ROAD

OAKLANDS

KERSAL
CELL

MANCHESTER
RACE
COURSE

THE
CLIFF

BURY NEW ROAD

DEVONSHIRE ST

see drawing below

River Irwell

GT CHEETHAM ST

CROMWELL RD

GERALD RD

BLANDFORD

dog
track

CAMP ST

CEDAR ST

RIGBY ST

GT CHEETHAM ST

BACK ROMAN ROAD

DEVONSHIRE ST

houses

shops

houses

FENNY ST

left
here

Knoll
House

Grove
Hotel

entered
here

surgery

BURY NEW ROAD

Rialto

to
Manchester

GROVE HOTEL

*Based on a map drawn in 1971 by Mr Bradshaw,
brother of Winifred Weatherby. See page 128.*

125

Joy Hancox indicating the priest hole under her house at Singleton Road in 1973

Top of the tunnel arch under the house on Singleton Road.

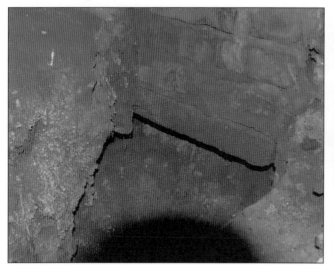

SINGLETON ROAD

While there are no further signs of an underground route beyond the grounds of Kersal Cell there is much more evidence of a tunnel running towards Manchester from Singleton Road to Cheetham. Joy Hancox found that her house, altered in 1923, was on the site of Broughton Hall Farm - the former home of, Tom Siddall, a prominent Jacobite activist. His father had been executed for his part in the 1715 Rebellion and Tom himself was beheaded in London after the 1745 uprising. The farm seems to have been a secret meeting place for the most fervent Jacobites and a refuge for those on the run. Siddall was also a member of a group known as the True British Catholic Church.

It was discovered during the installation of central heating in 1969 that beneath the house on Singleton Road, under the floorboards, there was a chamber with a flight of stone steps down to a brick wall. The old cellars were cleared to reveal partially stone-flagged floors, and amongst the 16 tons of rubble removed, a 1797 penny and old clay pipe were found. Further work

unearthed an old brick tunnel with a curved roof under the party wall. Descendants of the house builders revealed that they knew of the passage from the house which went under the road in the southerly direction towards Manchester. For reasons of safety the passage had been blocked off and filled with soil and rubble. The builders had also come across large flues which led to a 5ft 6in alcove behind a bedroom wall, which could have been a 'priest hole'.

The tunnel would have been an ideal way for Siddall and his friends to slip in and out of Manchester undetected. Siddall ran a barber's shop at Smithy Door, close to the Shambles. Sir Oswald Mosley, Lord of the Manor of Manchester appointed him 'Scavenger' of the Exchange district of the city, but after the Jacobite retreat he was pursued on his horse by a mob through the streets. They chased him down Market Street and into St Ann's square, where he dismounted and disappeared in the buildings. Had he escaped down the tunnel? He was later brought to justice and sentenced to death. After his execution, his head was brought back and publicly displayed on the Exchange.

BELLA VISTA

BETTY CROKE attended Broughton High School, which was in a large property formerly known as 'Bella Vista', on the corner of Broom Lane and Bury New Road. She remembers a tunnel under the school, which was accessed via the attic at the back of the house where she had French lessons. There was a cupboard in the room that was usually locked, but one particular day it was left open and she and her

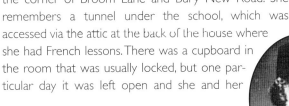

Sotorios Hazzopulo

friends found another low cupboard which was also unlocked. Inside were steps which led down into the cellar. Betty remembers being scared by the experience and that they were given detention.

Later the history teacher told her that the tunnel led directly to the cathedral, but it was now blocked off because of a road collapse and too dangerous to enter. It is not clear why there was an entrance to a tunnel from Bella Vista, which had been built on the site of a zoological garden. When it closed, some of the animals were given to Belle Vue Zoo.

There was also a tunnel from Bella Vista, previously the residence of Sotorios Hazzopulo, the Greek Consul to Manchester, to another Consulate, on Radford Street. Betty and her friends played here in a man-made cave in the old conservatory. The spot was to have national notoriety when in around 1944, a man abducted and tortured a child here. Afterwards the police blocked up the cave entrance. The house was later pulled down after vandalism.[1]

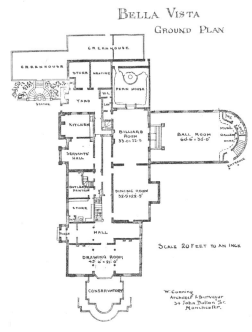

Plan of the house before its sale to the school

DEVONSHIRE STREET

MR J B DUNNE had a cousin who lived a few houses away from Devonshire Street on Bury New Road. The scullery floor subsided and revealed a cellar which had also collapsed, and below was an old passage, thought to run to the cathedral. The house was large with some interesting decorative features - bishop's mitres in each corner of a room and figures of the twelve Apostles in the hallway. It was in a group of houses demolished to build the Ascot Court flats. 1971 (JH)

'I can tell you for certain about a tunnel at Devonshire Street. When I was a little girl, about four years old, we lived at number four on the corner of Rigby Street and Devonshire Street. The house had ornamental religious sculptures in the garden and a miniature turreted wall. My brother's friend found a cellar with a bricked-up tunnel. I don't know why they didn't try to make a way through this around 1908. But I know my father said it was a tunnel going to the Cathedral, it supposedly started at Kersal Cell. We used to play in the ruins of Kersal Towers which was said to be connected with it. My sister says there was a priest hole above our dining room. There are now garages and flats where our house used to be.'
MRS FLYNN 1973 (JH)

MRS W WEATHERBY lived in Beaumont Street, Higher Broughton and at about the age of nine was dared by school friends to enter a supposedly haunted house on Devonshire Street. The row of houses were quite ornate with carvings of cherubs and saints on the stone porches. She went with six friends along with another twelve to make sure the dare was carried out. They scrambled down a grating at the front of the houses and through a broken window into a cellar which led to another without windows. They had a candle stub and a few matches to light the way.

There was an opening to another passage which they thought would lead back to the stairs, and so they went along in single file, holding hands. By this time she was at the end of the line, and she stumbled when the ground suddenly sloped steeply. The candle was lost in the con-fusion and she found herself with three others - voices could be heard but no-one answered their calls for help.

They decided to retrace their route - the boy behind her was hanging on to her long hair but they soon realised that they were lost. They huddled together on the floor, which was dry and solid but rather uneven. She remembered the air smelling earthy and it was stuffy. Eventually they were found as they heard men's voices and saw the light from their torches. Three policemen led them to safety and to her surprise they emerged out of a house on Bury New Road opposite the site of what would become the Rialto cinema.

The police had already made one fruitless search and then at the suggestion of her mother, they searched from the cellars of the Grove Inn. This was because she had some knowledge of the entrances of the underground passages, as when she was young, she had gone underground with her grandmother on a walk from Kersal Cell with a party of people to the Lady Chapel at Manchester Cathedral. She believed this tunnel had been an escape route for priests in troubled times. The floor was solid and it was tall enough for a man to stand upright. (1971 JH)

While there are eyewitness accounts on different sections of tunnel between Singleton Road and the Grove Inn on Bury New Road, there are no further references beyond this point into Manchester. A direct underground route would have to terminate at quite a distance from the cathedral otherwise there would be an immensely difficult engineering task of tunnelling beneath the River Irk.

There are two reports of tunnels in the Gerald Road area, Charlestown: J BERRY 1974 (JH) claimed that 'near Salford Dog Track, there was a stone cottage which had a passage running to the cathedral. My father went along this a few times. This also leads to Kersal Cell.' STAN PARKIN 6 September 1971 (JH) wrote that there was a tunnel from the racecourse to Gerald Road and the dog track, under a shop opposite Blandford Road. A tunnel heading towards either Kersal or Manchester would have to cross under the River Irwell. Mr Parkin also knew of 'a passage through a brick arch from Cedar Street which went about a quarter of a mile towards Manchester Race Course. There was a trickle of water down the middle'.

Salford 'underground' railway

The double-track line belonging to the Lancashire and Yorkshire Railway originally ran between the old Manchester Racecourse at New Barns and Windsor Bridge, with most of the mile and 104 yards route through tunnels. It opened in 1898, passing under the West Egerton Street Tunnel (471 yds) with a gradient of 1 in 47, Ellesmere Street Tunnel (291 yds) and West Park Tunnel (172yds) with a 1 in 68 gradient. Construction under this densely populated area involved underpinning many of the buildings above the tunnels.

The Racecourse had opened in 1876, replacing the course at Castle Irwell after its lease expired. The first Manchester November Handicap was held there that year with Polonaise the winner. Race horses were brought here by rail in special horse boxes.

The station was built on a gradient, with a platform on one side only, with assurances of a second platform from the railway company if the service developed.

In 1901 the course was closed and redeveloped as Number 9 Dock - the largest in the Docks - by the Manchester Ship Canal Company, opening in 1905. The line was extended towards the lower end of the docks and it became an important route taking goods to all parts of the country. The station was then known as 'Docks' and used by the dock construction workers, although the service was never advertised on public timetables.

At Windsor Bridge the railway linked to the Blackpool line, and Salford Docks Mission used the service for their annual children's outing. Up to four hundred children went on this trip each year until 1939. A newspaper article reported that this was the only passenger

Steps down to the station platform at Hulton Street.

West Egerton Street tunnel

Ellesmere Street tunnel

Former site of Manchester Race Course

New Park Street tunnel

New Barns station

trip along the line that year and so the station and platform had to be specially cleaned for the occasion. After this, it ceased to be used as a station, although it was briefly reopened for the transportation of war evacuees. [2] The former booking office, at the end of Race Street, had already become a mission hall and was still in use in 1969. There was a steep gradient from New Barns up to Windsor Bridge and so for safety reasons, only one train was allowed to be running on the line at any time. Locals were fascinated by the fleeting sight of the locomotives noisily steaming up and down the gradient, as they emerged from the tunnels.

Diesel shunters were used briefly before the closure of the line in 1963. Don Lee, footpaths rights of way campaigner, remembers walking the underground route after it ceased to be in operation. Although it was quite dark, there was enough light to make out the way without the use of a torch. By this time there were several railway trucks abandoned at the docks end. British Rail offered the land for sale but it was eventually acquired by Salford Council for £14,000. They were advised by engineers that it would not be practical to use it as a route for vehicles and so the tunnels were filled with rubble and the surface landscaped.

Woden's Cave

This was a huge cave in the red sandstone hill close to Oldfield Road, Ordsall, known also as 'Woden's Den'. It was so named because it was close to the ford and meadow belonging to a 'Wodarn'. The two local boundary names - 'Wodarnforde' and 'Wodarneleye' are first referred to in a charter of 1292. Before about 1770, 'Ordsall' was spelt either 'Wordsall' or 'Wordsal'.[3]

It has been claimed the cave had pagan or monastic associations, and it was described by Thomas Barritt as being ornamented with symbols, shields and crosses, including the barely visible image of a shield with a sword handle across it. His drawing of the cave in 1780

appears to show two entrances. However, later observers have queried his dimension of the cave and its use, and it is more likely that the 'cave' was a quarry for the nearby Ordsall Hall. J Owen recalled blocks of red sandstone there around 1830.[4]

James Hall, a Quaker dyer, bought the land containing the 'cave' in 1808 for his house 'Sunnyside' on Ordsall Hill. He had the entrances of the cavern filled in to deter visitors. All trace of the site was obliterated with the coming of the railway, but it was located on the site of the present day Woden's Avenue.

The tower, built around 1895, is a ventilation shaft in the grounds of Salford University. There is an air duct which connects to the basement of the former Salford School of Technology building where there was a weaving shed. A child was thought to have fallen down the shaft in late 1970s.

Manchester underground rail plans

Manchester has made many attempts to construct an underground rail network, dating back to 1839, when there were plans for a tunnel to link the lines which approached from five directions. It involved the building of a station at Hunts Bank to connect to the Birmingham line via a tunnel to Store Street. However this project was blocked by those with canal shareholdings, who saw their financial interests threatened, and argued that a station should be more centrally placed in the vicinity of Piccadilly.

In 1868 the Council considered a proposal for a route from Mount Street off Albert Square, emerging in the open near Whitworth Park and passing through Rusholme, Fallowfield and Didsbury at the corner of Didsbury Park and Wilmslow Road. (London's first underground line opened in 1863).

There was a proposal to introduce a parliamentary bill in 1878 for the construction of an underground railway to run from the north side of Blackfriars Street, under Deansgate, St Mary's Gate, Market Street, and terminating in a plot of vacant land on the north side of Piccadilly.

'Manchester is at last to have its own tube railway'

1903

In 1903 a scheme was presented but outvoted, and then in 1912 it was announced that 'Manchester is at last to have its own tube railway' but the First World War brought an end to the project. In 1927 a scheme with an inner circle of stations and lines branching to five districts was presented. This was amended the following year to just the inner circle of seven underground stations connecting with main line and suburban services, and it seemed to be coming to a successful outcome. Councillor T Walker, Chairman of the Underground Railway Committee said in 1930 'Manchester will start boring its underground railway this year. That is a declaration, I can make it with the utmost confidence'. Unfortunately his confidence was misplaced because the government would not give the estimated 75% needed of the £11 million cost.

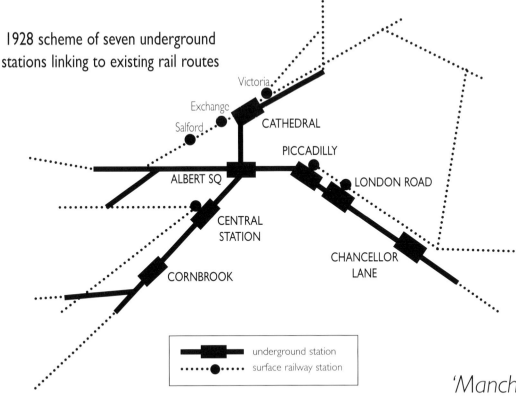

1928 scheme of seven underground stations linking to existing rail routes

Victoria

Exchange

Salford

CATHEDRAL

PICCADILLY

ALBERT SQ

LONDON ROAD

CENTRAL
STATION

CHANCELLOR
LANE

CORNBROOK

underground station
surface railway station

Professor Miles Walker, formerly of the Manchester College of Technology, commenting on the city's transport problems in 1933 said *'Manchester communications are thoroughly obsolete. Anyone who has lived in the city knows the dreadful waste of time that occurs every day when its inhabitants try to get from one part to another. Add up all that waste of time and lost temper during the last ten years and you have enough cause to build an underground railway several times over'*.

Nevertheless, despite the professor's comments, schemes in 1934 and 1936 foundered due to high costs, although Alderman Bowie, who championed the proposal thought that the tunnels had the additional value of being a place of safety from aerial attacks during wartime. This was met with laughter by some at a council meeting and the Alderman replied 'You never know'. This scheme involved scrapping the three existing mainline stations - London Road (Piccadilly), Victoria and Central, and building a new overground City Station at Gaythorn which linked with new underground stations - Mayfield, Piccadilly Exchange and New Cross. Around eight miles of

'Manchester will start boring its underground railway this year. That is a declaration, I can make it with the utmost confidence'

1930

new railway, mostly underground, would be required. Bowie dismissed objections that the system would interfere with the coal mines stating that the rail tunnels would be at no more than 40 feet depth.

There was another council investigation in 1939 which came to nothing, but immediately after the war interest briefly revived in a possible underground system. The Post War Planning Committee investigated the possibilities and claimed that the costs were prohibitive, congestion may not be relieved and, controversially, 'there was no demand'.

Further proposals were presented in 1948, 1955, 1963 and then by British Rail in 1966. There was more encouragement in 1968, when the City Council gave permission for detailed feasibility studies to be carried out. A system was investigated for an 11-mile line from Northenden to Higher Blackley with a branch line to East Didsbury. By 1971 this had been revised to an underground link between Piccadilly and Victoria Stations at a cost of £40 million. The following year Parliamentary approval was obtained for the proposed link,

Below left: Manchester Rapid Transit Study 1968, with the line entering the south side of the city centre via Oxford Road Station

Right: The 1970 Picc-Vic line proposal

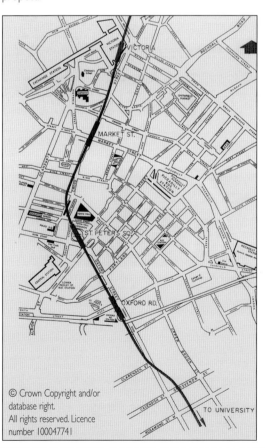

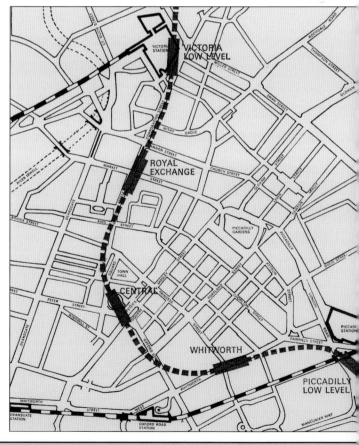

which was to be 2.75 miles long, running from Ardwick Junction to Queen's Road Junction on the Bury line. Just over two miles of the line would be in the tunnel, which would be 60-70 feet beneath the City centre. Electric trains would run at a frequency of two and a half minute intervals. There were to be five new central stations - Piccadilly Low level, Whitworth, Central, Royal Exchange and Victoria Low Level, with a target date for completion as 1978.[5]

Engineering test bores along the route did not reveal any insurmountable problems, despite the presence of the West Manchester Fault which ran close to part of the route, nor coal mining subsidence at the northern end from the Bradford Colliery which was due to close. No mention was made of any other underground workings - such as Guardian Underground Tunnel which although crossing the route of Picc-Vic, would have been further below ground.

Work on the Arndale Shopping Centre began in 1972 with space underground allocated for one of the stations, and various reports included detailed plans. It is sometimes claimed that the platforms for Royal Exchange Station under the Arndale were actually completed, but this is dismissed as incorrect today by people who were involved in the project.

Test bore

Manchester Archives & Local Studies

Between 1973 and 1975 the Government announced various grant cuts and decision delays which resulted in the £156 million Picc-Vic scheme being halted. It was noted that slightly less ambitious tunnels were being finished in Newcastle and Liverpool. The scheme was officially abandoned in July 1977 and Manchester was forced to consider cheaper options, which eventually resulted in the overground Metrolink tram system. Some have questioned whether the presence of the nuclear bunker was the real reason for the Picc-Vic's cancellation, but the correspondence between Government and Manchester leaders indicates that it was economics that drove the decision. Also having recently talked to a member of the working party of engineers and planners on the scheme, I conclude that 'Guardian' was never part of their considerations.[6]

For the time being, all thought of an underground system has been put aside as the Metrolink tram network begins to expand, but history suggests that at some time in the future others will begin to dream of the day when the city finally gets its long awaited underground railway.

The mysterious William Connell

He seemed
to have
the 'knowledge'
about
underground
Manchester

Following her article on tunnels around Manchester in the *Manchester Evening News* in 1973, Joy Hancox received many helpful letters on the subject. People wrote about passages they had personally explored, or had been told about - many of the recollections are included in this book. But one letter written in January 1973 stood out from all the others. Not only was it quite specific about locations, but also the writer seemed to have first-hand experience of tunnels. But even more interesting, the correspondent claimed to know the whereabouts of a complete tunnel network around Greater Manchester. He said the tunnels were linked and that they ran right into the heart of the City. The information contained details that Joy Hancox had never seen before. Could it be substantiated? What else could be found out from the writer? Here was a possible rich vein of information for a tunnel researcher. He seemed to have the 'knowledge' about underground Manchester. Joy wanted to know more and so she got in contact with William Connell.

The result was a series of meetings and an exchange of correspondence which went on until his death in 1988. The information he passed on was sometimes borne out by other letter writers and contacts, or proved by research, but on other occasions he told her things, the authenticity of which to this day, we are not completely sure of. The quality of his information was on another level from that of others - what are we to make of it? What we decide, will form our conclusions about what lies below Manchester.

The reason for this reticence about his information stems from the behaviour and known associations of William Connell. Although in some parts of his life he seemed to lead a normal existence working for the local council and the GPO, in other ways he had connections which made Joy wary of his motives and caused her to consider carefully the complete truth of his tunnel stories.

When Joy first met with Connell at his home in Didsbury in 1973, he seemed rather nervous. She noted the contrast between his expensive glasses and radio, and the sparsely-furnished accommodation. He was very thin and fragile, possibly still suffer-

Joy Hancox

ing the after effects of a spinal operation three years previously, which meant he could not stand for long periods. He spent the entire meeting fidgeting with a cigarette which he never got to light.

Between 1923 and 1933 he had worked for the Manchester Corporation Electricity Board as a junior electrical engineer, and then for ten years from 1953 with the GPO - ideal jobs to get to know about what lies below the city streets. When he was fifteen, he had explored the tunnels with a friend. It was an adventure to them and they had gone equipped with bicycle lamps, and oil lamps, and took readings by compass. He recalled an amazing journey when they travelled the whole length of a tunnel close to the Cathedral, under Market Street and Piccadilly, eventually squeezing through iron railings in Reddish Vale. No estimate of dimensions was given but he described the tunnel as wide and high. The floor was compacted earth, and the walls and arched roof were made of stone. Other tunnels which he had only partly explored were of similar dimensions and construction. The air was still but not stale and there were no draughts. He was adamant that all the tunnels linked at a point near, but not underneath the cathedral, and that they were not to be confused with the remains of old submerged city streets, or sewers and drains.

Connell claimed he walked beneath Market Street.

Conversations with Connell were not always easy - he could be evasive, sometimes declining to say any more, and then at other times provide fresh information without prompting. On more than one occasion he was dismissive of anyone publishing a book on underground Manchester, saying that no-one would be interested in things of the past, and that it would be better to write a romantic novel or about an aspect of Roman history - in other words: stay off Manchester tunnels!

In a 1980s letter, after a period of much redevelopment in Manchester, when he said many tunnels had been obliterated, he thought that would be the end of interest in the subject. Why did it matter to him if it was made public? After all it was he who had first written to Joy. Rather mysteriously, Connell said he had written to her 'to give her a clue', and that she was free to use the content of his letter in any way she chose. He gave the impression he knew more than he was admitting - there was always another snippet of information after claiming he could say no more. Also he gave the impression he was both trying to establish how much Joy knew on the subject, and discouraging the writing of a book .

Perhaps a clue to Connell's thinking lay in his own revelations about his time during the last war. He had not been on military service but had been given special dispensation to chauffeur Sir Hartley Shawcross, who was in charge of defences for North West England, and HD Moorhouse who directed Manchester's civil defence. Connell owned two Chrysler cars and was allowed unlimited petrol coupons for the job, although he was never officially paid. He said he visited a secret war-time underground munitions factory, producing machine bullets, located beneath a lake in Crumpsall Vale, as well as various anti-aircraft sites.

After the war he continued to have many contacts in Manchester, mentioning he had worked on the nuclear bunker. He had also been in touch with the builders of the Arndale Centre to indicate where tunnels and shafts were located, and then talked of working with a local MP on an unspecified matter. A 1980 letter stated that although he had a flat in Didsbury, he did not spend all his time there and he would make future arrangements to meet by telephone.

The Shambles, in its original site off Market Place, once an access point to a tunnel.

He remembered a road collapse under New Brown Street*, caused by a tunnel. The subsidence was of such vast proportions that repair work took six months, with a permanent watchman kept on site. Other subsidence at Hanging Ditch, Deansgate, Withy Grove and Corporation Street seemed significant to him. He had come across dozens of short tunnels in the area around the Cathedral but they were frequently bricked up. Other places were mentioned as gateways to a tunnel network including the Old Boar's Head, the Shambles off Old Market Place, Liston's Music Hall and Ellis Brigham's in the Corn Exchange.

*This is thought to be a 1930s telephone duct between Spring Gardens and Thompson House - now the Print Works

During the building of the Arndale Centre, part of Market Street collapsed because of a tunnel below and Connell went down and witnessed concrete being poured into the hole. When Kendals built the subway beneath Deansgate, they broke into the old Deansgate tunnel which ran from Hunts Bank to the Bridgewater Canal at Old Trafford. Another tunnel ran from Hunts Bank via Piccadilly to All Saints.

Connell gave an account of going along a tunnel under the old Horsfall Museum in Ancoats. He recalled pushing his arms through an iron grille at the museum, to reach into a bran tub and pull out a ticket advertising an event. He also told a macabre story from the 1920's when he worked for the electricity board. A team of men were working near Withy Grove and Greenwood Street when one of the other workmen became hysterical. He kept shouting 'she's beautiful, she's blue'. They thought the man was deranged and he was taken away to Prestwich Hospital. However when Connell went to look at the trench where the man had been digging, he found an opened lead-lined coffin in which lay the body of a beautiful young girl with a blue face already turning brown with the influx of air. The coffin was removed to a warehouse across the road where other 'found' coffins were stored.

In 1974, after much persuasion, he agreed to take part in two broadcasts for Granada Television's 'Scene at Six Thirty', with Joy Hancox, visiting underground sites with presenter Brian Trueman. Connell

William Connell with Joy Hancox and Brian Trueman in the Victoria Arches during the production of the Granada programme.

Joy Hancox

seemed genuinely to remember his first visit to the Victoria Arches and was able to point out the location of nearby streets.

The information Connell gave over the years, generally confirms the accounts given by others and leads me to give some credence to his other claims of a wider tunnel network. Many of the details which he provided can be verified. Also, the main facts he gave over the years did not substantially alter when he retold stories. It would be difficult to maintain and remember a made up-story over a long period. He was uncertain about the origins of the underground routes although he would often refer to them as the 'Roman tunnels'. The impression was given that government or local authority agencies were interested in the network possibly for civil defence reasons. He seemed genuinely sorry that from the 1970s, many of the old tunnels were being obliterated by property developers whom he considered had no interest in Manchester's past.

Joy Harcox

William Connell points to where he remembered an exit from the arches.

But mystery still surrounds Connell. He claimed to have been born in Edinburgh in 1908, lived at Gravesend and Toxteth, near Canterbury, and then later with an uncle in Sheffield. By his own admission he had never raised a family, he lived alone in a sparsely-furnished flat. Was that his real home or did he have another place? He thought of himself as someone easy to get on with, but was anxious not to be seen as 'a mug'. Even though he made himself known to Joy Hancox and passed on lots of tunnel information, his motives for doing this and the details of who he worked for are not entirely clear. Not everything he said has been confirmed - in particular, the routes from the vales, and the Crumpsall Vale munitions site remain a puzzle. I am aware that a common technique of those who wish to mislead or confuse will be to integrate enough truth in a story to make it sound convincing. It would seem fair to say that whatever reservations there may be about William Connell, his information is worthy of further investigation, and seems to have helped further our knowledge of underground Manchester. He died in Didsbury in 1988.

See 'WILLIAM CONNELL REVISITED' by JOY HANCOX, page 152

Four Tunnels

Tuesday 23rd January '73

With regard to the news item in Wednesday's Evening News, and your own item on 'Manchester's Underground'.

I had some experience of these tunnels in the early Twenties and can tell you that the group of four tunnels originally ran to the four vales which surround Manchester - Crumpsall, Endam (Queensway Cheetham), Clayton & Reddish.

Another tunnel ran from this group, across the front of the Cathedral, (With an entrance, or outlet, on the riverside at Hunt's Bank) along Deansgate, and on to the side of the Bridgewater Canal, near the swing-bridge at Trafford Park.

The Reddish Vale tunnel runs under Market Street, under the back of Lewis's; under the new Piccadilly Hotel, and on in what I could only judge to be a straight line to Reddish Vale, emerging under what was then, an old railway line.

If I remember correctly, a proposed extension to Lewis's, (in the Twenties) was abandoned on account of this tunnel.

Each of the tunnels which I fully explored, Reddish and Cornbrook, had an iron gate at the end, was quite dry, and wide enough for a single-line rail-way, there were also plenty of rats at both ends, but none along the length.

I only partly explored the other tunnels but was satisfied by compass reading that they went in the right direction, and I have seen the Clayton Vale end of what I feel sure was one of these tunnels.

Faithfully ,
William Connell, , West Didsbury, M20 8NN

The intriguing letter from William Connell

Joy Hancox

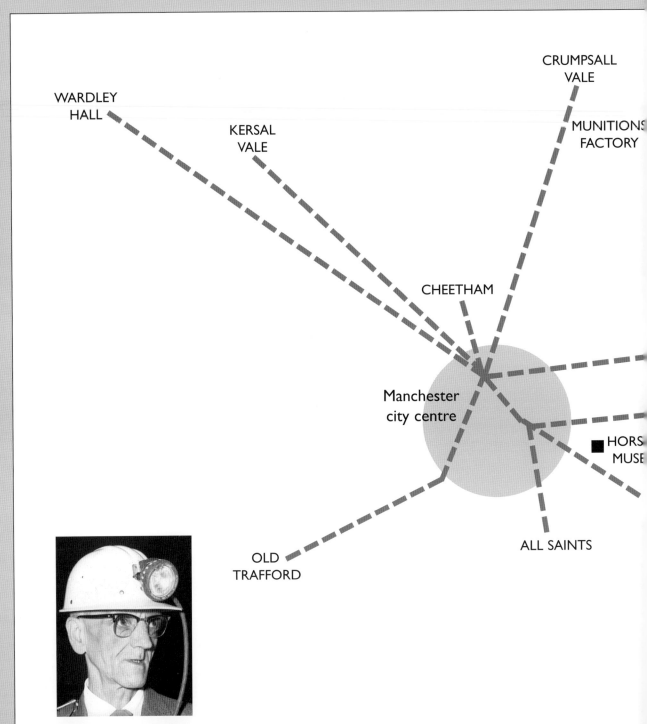

CRUMPSALL VALE

MUNITIONS FACTORY

WARDLEY HALL

KERSAL VALE

CHEETHAM

Manchester city centre

HORS MUSE

ALL SAINTS

OLD TRAFFORD

William Connell's tunnels

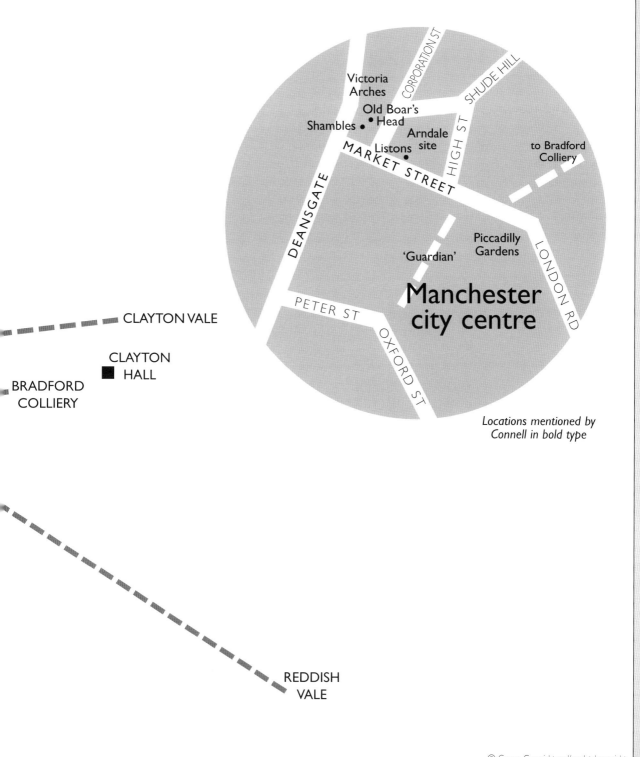

Victoria
Arches

CORPORATION ST

SHUDE HILL

Old Boar's
• Head

Shambles •

Arndale
site

HIGH ST

to Bradford
Colliery

Listons
•

MARKET STREET

DEANSGATE

'Guardian'

Piccadilly
Gardens

LONDON RD

Manchester
city centre

PETER ST

OXFORD ST

CLAYTON VALE

CLAYTON
■ HALL

BRADFORD
COLLIERY

*Locations mentioned by
Connell in bold type*

REDDISH
VALE

Rumours of tunnels
and treasure

CATEATON STREET

S CROWDER was told by a taxi driver colleague that below Cateaton Street there was an old cobbled street, complete with old houses and shops with bay windows, but in a dilapidated state. It was not possible to go more than a few yards because it was infested with rats. (1974 JH)

Cateaton Street

FARMERS' TUNNEL

It seems that in early Manchester there was a large underground cavern at St Mary's Gate, Deansgate, which was so cold that it was used as a meat storage house and slaughterhouse. The local residents of that time were so upset by the mess caused by the cattle which were herded from the outskirts by local farmers that they pressed the elders of the town to pass a by-law forbidding the moving of livestock other than by cart into the centre of Manchester.

The mess the residents complained about was not so much the mess of the main street, Market Stead Lane, but the fouling of the town's water supply, which was drawn from an artesian well in Spring Gardens and ran in wooden troughs along the main street.

The farmers of the day were quite poor and could not afford the cartage charges, so they formed a type of working party with the farm workers to dig a subway from Ardwick to Manchester, this being a distance of about three miles. After several starts and failures a tunnel was eventually started and finished in 14 months.

This tunnel runs from somewhere near Ardwick Green Park, under the Co-op at Downing Street, on towards Piccadilly Station and follows roughly the path taken by Store Street, Jutland Street, Hilton Street and Smithfield Market and came up somewhere around the Cathedral.

The tunnel was a success until the town's elders clamped a toll tax on any person using this tunnel, this being almost as much as the charge for transport. This proved a crippling blow to the farmers, who hardly ever used the passages after this.

K J B   MANCHESTER EVENING NEWS 1967

HOUGH HALL

The Tudor farmhouse still exists today in Moston, and it is claimed that Bonnie Prince Charlie hid there while he was being pursued by the English army in 1745. He was said to have taken refuge at the Old Boars Head at Middleton and then came to the hall. As the attackers closed in, he escaped through a secret tunnel which led to a nearby farm house at a place later known as Harpurhey Tip.

HULME HALL

A tradition states that a subterranean passage ran under the river from Hulme Hall to the Cathedral. An arched opening in the cliff, according to tradition, led to a subterranean chamber where several treasures were said to have been hidden by the Dowager Lady Prestwich and never recovered in consequence of her immediate decease. It is well known that the hall was approached from the north by an old bridge crossing the Medlock, which here empties itself into the Irwell. Near the hall were the meadows where the late Mr Leo Grindon loved to collect the spring crocuses but all these have vanished now. Railways are sad destroyers of beauty and nature. Hulme Hall Lane now cuts through the site of the old mansion towards Salford, whilst the Altrincham Railway crosses it overhead.
FL. TAVARE CITY NEWS 1915

Overhanging the river in front of the hall, was the red sandstone 'Fisherman's Rock' - a popular spot for anglers. The space below the rock was known as ''Robber's Cave'

The legend of Hulme Hall referred to by Tavare states that Sir Thomas Prestwich, Lord of Hulme had been assured by his mother that she had treasure for him hidden somewhere around Hulme Hall. But, a sudden illness caused her to lose the power of speech and she was unable to tell him the whereabouts of the treasure before she died. Later Prestwich's Royalist sympathies led him to be fined £313 and he had to mortgage the Hulme Hall estate to the Mosley family of Ancoats who eventually came to own it.[1]

Hulme Hall was situated at Cornbrook close to the River Irwell at the end of Hulme Hall Road.

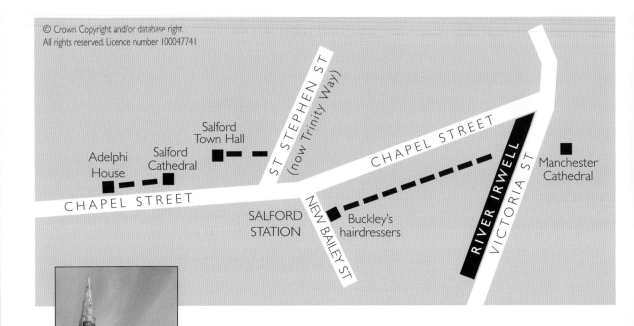

Salford Cathedral

Salford's former Town Hall

SALFORD TO MANCHESTER

EDNA DOODSON NEE JONES a triplet who was brought up in Salford, says it was common knowledge that there was a tunnel linking Adelphi House, and Salford Cathedral.

BERNARD WEBSTER, who worked as an engineer for Manchester Council, knew of a tunnel between Salford Town Hall and St Stephen Street. (JH)

MISS S KENNEDY'S uncle had a barber's shop on New Bailey Street, opposite Salford Station *(Buckley's hairdressers ?)*. He told her that there was a passage from his cellar to Manchester Cathedral.
(June 1971 JH)

SIR HUMPHREY CHETHAM HOTEL

MRS D M BUTTERWORTH was about ten when her parents moved to the Sir Humphrey Chetham Hotel in Clayton in 1888. Her mother told her that in the cellars were passages with archways leading into other passages which led to St Cross Church, Chetham's School and the Cathedral. (JH)

Smedley Lodge

SMEDLEY HALL

MRS WALLACE'S uncle broke up a tunnel in the grounds of Smedley Hall which was said to lead to the Cathedral.
(1973 JH)

The tunnel referred to may have been the 'Old Roman dungeon' in the grounds where it was thought an area of level ground was used for jousting, with spectators watching from the terraces.

Memories of the Inspector of sewers

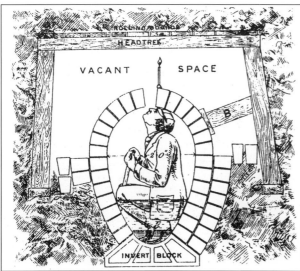

INSPECTOR WILKINSON featured in a Manchester Evening News article when he retired after forty-five years' service in 1938. He had spent most of his working life underground, working in the narrow passages under the city, and knew the whereabouts of all the underground rivers and springs. Sometimes he had made headlong dashes for his life as sudden surges of water foamed at his feet. 'You have to make for the nearest ladder, hoist yourself as near as you can to the roof in the hope that the water will eventually subside'. Accumulated gases were another danger.

It could be dangerous work and he considered that every time he went underground he was risking his life. When he first started work in the department, the sewers were cramped narrow tunnels in which he had to crawl along. There were just a few places to take refuge if the heavy rains flooded through. But the Inspector had supervised the construction of new tunnels, including one at Blackfriars, which were big enough to drive a lorry through.

During one tour of sewer examination his torch light picked out 'two big fiercely luminous eyes in the darkness'. He drew back when he felt the lunge of some sort of wild animal and heard a snarl. Further inspection revealed a cat that had grown wild and vicious after spending months in the darkness hunting rats. Wilkinson and other colleagues had to go back armed with weapons and protective clothing to drive out the cat into the river via an outlet. When he came across around two hundred rats he shouted loudly to frighten them off.

Manchester sewermen Patrick Lavin and James Burns in 1960

Tree root penetration in the Lord Exerton sewer

Store Street sewer collapse

Openshaw sewers completed in 1973

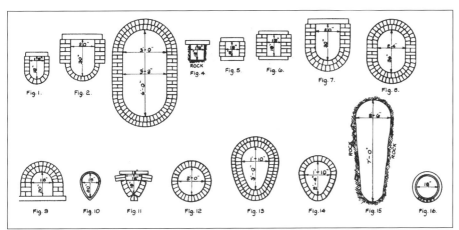

Early 19th century varieties of sewer cross sections

William Connell revisited

By JOY HANCOX

When I decided to give the author access to the material I had gathered about tunnels under Manchester, it was already clear that the information supplied by William Connell stood out from all the rest. Some years had passed since my first meeting with Connell and distance brought an objectivity from which I was able to re-examine what he told me about himself as well as the underground of the city. Accordingly I set about filling in some of the gaps in his personal history that had always been a matter of concern. At the time I felt I had done what I could.

I had already obtained a copy of his death certificate. It shows clearly that he died on 21st June, 1988 in Withington Hospital, Manchester. There is no mystery, then, about that. But what of his birth? The death certificate gives the date and place as 13th September 1908, Manchester. This conflicts with his statement to me that he had been born in Edinburgh. Which was true ?

.Enquiries in Scotland produced no record of his birth there. When I looked for him in Manchester I made an interesting and unexpected discovery. One that seems now to typify so much about this man. The birth appears to have been first registered in1923, not 1908 although there is a reference to a birth in 1908 on the document. Strangely, Manchester Register Office have no birth for a William Connell in 1908 recorded in their Index. There is no official documentation attesting to the first fourteen and a half years of his life. Certainly his surname was Connell in 1923. Had it been Connell before then ? 1923 was the year Connell claimed he started to work for Manchester Corporation Electricity Board as a junior electrical engineer. I had already traced and spoken to a colleague who remembered working with him. So in 1923 William Connell would have needed some proof of identity to start on his employment and that 'proof' appears to be in this late registration of the birth that is tantamount to an adoption. During our many conversations he repeatedly referred to himself as a 'loner' without a family of his own, although he claimed that he got on with everyone. But he did on one memorable occasion tell me quite decidedly but not in a boastful way that he was a member of the 'Wills' family, the famous tobacco dynasty that hailed from Bristol and became such generous benefactors to that city. I did not pursue his claim at the time because it did not seem relevant. I was too interested in working out the map of his underground journeys in Manchester. Now I have been through my notes and his correspondence yet again and noticed that he signed himself in two letters towards the end of his life in 1980 as 'E. Wm. Connell'. His earlier letters and his death certificate have no 'E' and no hints of any Christian name other than William.

Beaumont Street, Beswick

The Manchester Register Office was able to produce a birth certificate for one Ernest William Connell from the same registration district (Prestwich) and for the same birth date shown on William Connell's death certificate - 13th September 1908. The mother's name on this certificate was given as Beatrice Bessie Wills. These fresh details seemed to confirm the claim made to me almost in passing all those years ago in 1973.

At last I was beginning to fill in those missing earlier years in the young Connell's life. It was the additional name of Ernest that provided the clue. The name of his father on the 1908 certificate is George William Connell. He was evidently a 'private' in the army based at Chatham Barracks when he married Beatrice Bessie Wills on 25th September 1905. He was twenty-four, she was eighteen. The marriage took place in the Register Office at Strood, Kent, by special licence.

According to the public records Ernest William Connell was born at 82 Beaumont Street, Beswick, North Manchester on 13th September 1908. Judging from an examination of the surrounding streets in Slater's Directory for that year and subsequent ones there was a close-knit family group of Connells living in the area. It was to these that George and Beatrice gravitated. George's own father, Oliver, was a brick-seller.

Both his parents disappear from these records and a likely explanation may be that William's father was killed in World War One and that his mother, like so many other widows of that war, remarried out of necessity and then died still young. That would square with Connell's own childhood memories of a nomadic existence with an 'uncle' and finally leaving this uncle in Sheffield to return to the Connell family roots in Manchester as a teenager. Here James and Mary Connell gave him a degree of stability and official identity at the age of fourteen and a half. Hence the second certificate for 'William' in 1923 - the year he started work in Manchester and the year of his first recorded tunnel escapade in the course of that work. Whether his surviving papers included either of his birth certificates is not known, but either his mother or someone else must have told him of her links with the Wills family. It was not a connection he chose to renew. Yet in his senior years, at the age of seventy-two, he decided to introduce the 'E' briefly into his signature. It would seem that his mother turned her back on the family in marrying 'beneath' her but told the young boy something of her early life before she died.

Her marriage certificate states that Beatrice Bessie Wills was the daughter of Charles William Wills (deceased) who is described as 'Foreman Cement Works'. A careful check of earlier public documents records that he was at one time a 'reader' (presumably a proof reader) for a newspaper in London. He was brought up in Southwark and was the son of William H. Wills, then working in the tobacco business.

One William Henry Wills became first Baron Winterstoke in 1906. He was the first chairman of Imperial Tobacco and a prominent member of the wealthy British tobacco importing company of Wills. He was a generous benefactor to the City of Bristol where his brother, Henry Overton Wills, became the first chancellor of the University.

There is no suggestion that Beatrice was the grand daughter of this particular William Henry Wills, but there is every indication that she was a member of the extensive Wills tobacco dynasty based in Bristol. Their philanthropy in both the nineteenth and early twentieth centuries is a matter of record. That philanthropy included employment of less fortunate members of the Wills family.

Joy Hacox with William Connell and Brian Trueman during the making of the Granada TV programme on underground Manchester

Joy Hancox

William Connell's casual remark about a family connection with the Wills family made me reconsider other names he had mentioned in conversation. His tin of tobacco and strange little habit of rolling his own cigarettes took on a new significance. That he never smoked the cigarette only increased my curiosity.

There were three distinct periods when Connell learned about Manchester underground. First there was his time with the Corporation's former Electricity Board from 1923 to 1933. Then came his service in wartime Manchester and finally his work with the GPO between 1953 and 1963. I learned little of the years between 1933 and the beginning of the war but by 1939 he told me he was the proud owner of two Chrysler cars, one of which was commandeered like so many other private vehicles at the time for use by the military during the war. I gathered from remarks scattered through our conversations that he had built up a private hire service for a somewhat exclusive clientele. From the 1923 certificate I learned that his 'adoptive' father, James, had worked for a 'coach painter' and that may have been the original source of his contacts with the local

Midland Hotel

motor car trade. Be that as it may, when war came his conscription into the army was replaced by the job of chauffeuring important figures in the civil defence around Manchester and visiting stars from ENSA, the Entertainments National Service Association who provided entertainment for the armed forces during the war.

One of the people mentioned in connection with his wartime work was Lord Colwyn. This man made his fortune as a rubber and cotton manufacturer, became Deputy Chairman of Martin's Bank Ltd. and a director of several railway companies. He also owned a considerable property in Manchester city centre. He was a member of Manchester's exclusive Clarendon Club, now defunct but once a favourite haunt for the aristocracy in the region. It was no doubt Colwyn who employed Connell to move money around the city banks in his car, a precursor of today's Securicor service. Colwyn owned property in Market street and Connell regaled me with the story of how on one occasion his lordship found it necessary to break into one of his own offices and called on Connell for his help. It became clear to me that in a variety of roles William Connell became known to and trusted by some very influential figures in Manchester.

Perhaps the most important of these was Sir Hartley Shawcross, Attorney General in Clement Attlee's post-war government, perhaps best remembered now as the leader of the British team of prosecutors at the Nuremberg trials of the Nazis. In 1942 he was appointed 'Commissioner for the North West' with overall responsibility for defence in the region. Connell was his chauffeur in Manchester, collecting him from and delivering him to the Midland Hotel.

It was in the bar of the Midland, but before the war, that Connell met another figure who was to gain notoriety as the last man executed in Britain for treason. This was William Joyce. In the 1930s the decline of Manchester's cotton industry and wide unemployment made Manchester a target for Sir Oswald Mosley and his party of black-shirted fascists. For a while Joyce acted as Mosley's right-hand man in the region until they fell out and Mosley sacked him. Joyce was becoming increasingly extreme and violent in his views and fled to Germany a month before war broke out. From there he broadcast Nazi propaganda regularly to Britain hoping to undermine the country's fighting spirit. Connell appears to have met him early in his political career. Sir Oswald Mosley destined to become a political pariah himself was, of course, the descendant of the earlier Mosleys of Ancoats Hall, the former Lords of the Manor of Manchester. He came to the city to open the headquarters of his British Union of Fascists in North Manchester. It is only recently that I discovered those headquarters were housed at 17, Northumberland Street. This large mansion lay in almost a direct line with the tunnel going from Singleton Road, under the old school at Bella Vista, Devonshire Street and the site of the former Grove Inn. The mansion has long been replaced by a Synagogue. It is an ironic twist of Fate and an appropriate one that the headquarters of a movement once riddled with anti-Semitism has made way for a centre for devout Jewish studies and worship.

Joy Hancox and William Connell

I reflected on these facts. Thomas Siddall had tenanted the farm where my own house now stands. He had been employed as a 'Scavenger' for the Oswald Mosley of his day. Ancoats Hall had given way to the Horsfall Museum and that, too, has now gone. 17, Northumberland Street and Bella Vista have likewise disappeared from the landscape. But we must be careful not to lose sight of the history associated with vanished landmarks. Connell, although a private individual, was taken down the now defunct Bradford Colliery by a local miner and walked underground all the way to Piccadilly Gardens in the city centre. Such testimony is valuable for many reasons.

Perhaps William Connell, on reading the article about my interest in tunnels and seeing the map, knowing, too, so much about what lay under the city had been urged by an impulse to help me preserve some of that history when he wrote his first tantalising letter. If that is so, he has served the city well that took him in as a teenager.

Final thoughts

It is not within the scope of this book to make too many firm conclusions regarding the tunnel system beneath the City. My aim has been to draw attention to the 'evidence' regarding their existence. As this underground network will be a surprise to most, there will be many more questions regarding its origin and purpose, but it is possible to make several observations.

We know that the present street levels in the City are much higher than they were centuries ago. This is evidenced at the Mitre Hotel by the Cathedral, where the cellars reveal arching from a previous street around eight or ten feet below ground. From the 1770s there was a series of road improvement acts which both widened thoroughfares and raised levels. For example an 1821 Act, affecting at least nine streets, required Market Street to be widened to twenty yards and others to sixteen. In later working, there is an account of the level of Market Street between Brown Street and the Exchange being raised by eight feet.[1] This could have involved a series of supporting arches within this newly created underground space. So present day Manchester's street levels date back to around the 1840s.

Market Street before widening

Although there is documentation about the two canal tunnels under Deansgate and Whitworth Street, and Victoria Arches, there is nothing on the industrial workings around Ardwick, or the network of other routes beneath the city. The gathered evidence in this book points to the existence of tunnels beneath Deansgate and what is now known as New Cathedral Walk. The vicinity of Victoria Arches seemed to be the hub of an underground network which also went to Shude Hill, Cannon Street, and Market Street. It seems possible it extended to Cross Street, and to Ancoats. These tunnels, which seem to be Victorian in origin and intended as sewers, went beyond the city to the surrounding vales. By the time they were explored in the 1940s, by William Connell and Norman Savory, they seemed relatively dry and unused.

The continuing redevelopment of the city means that it is increasingly difficult to trace the remains of old Manchester. But there are fascinating glimpses of the past still to be found. Bob Bonner remembers during his time in the fire service, going down into the basement of a store on Market Street where part of the remains of one of the old courts, which used to be a feature of the area, could be seen. Within this enclosed basement space, an old 'no parking' sign remained on the wall. Work still goes on to undercover Manchester's underground past. For example, progress is still being made in tracing the extent of the tunnel from the Grocers' Wharf at Castlefield, with the recent discovery of a shaft.

Shaft discovered on the line of the Grocers' Warehouse tunnel

There have been many tunnel myths regarding Manchester. People talk about a Post Office underground transportation system but I have found no evidence of its existence. Suggestions of an underground route between the Midland Hotel and Central Station are unproven, as are the tales of underground streets and shops in the city. While it is possible for an old street to exist, no-one has so far provided details of the location. Stories of a 'lost' tube station below the Arndale Centre are also untrue. Speculation about a tunnel net-

The Victoria Arches, a key underground space

Old plans of cellars extending beyond the walls of a building on Market Street, which demonstrate how much underground space can be created.

United Utilities

work within the 'Guardian' nuclear bunker bigger than previously reported would seem unfounded, although for obvious security reasons, the locations and extent of access points are not known.

There are a number of descriptions of tunnels from childhood, which I can accept, but I am more wary when the stories come from their parents. Were these stories made up to impress or even frighten? Perhaps these were tales passed down through the generations. Fear of the unknown will often produce speculation and half-truth.

As we review this information about what lies below the streets, not only do we begin to see the possibilities of further exploration and research, but also start to think how these areas could be opened up to the public. Guides already organise 'Underground Manchester' walks around the City centre, which take visitors along canal towpaths, but there are many more tourism opportunities. There is, of course, the 'Underground Manchester' permanent exhibition at the Manchester Museum of Science and Industry, which imaginatively traces the history of the city's water supply and sanitation. Here the visitor walks through a reconstructed sewer, sees a Roman latrine, and experiences the sights, sounds and smells of Victorian Manchester.

But there is so much more of interest to experience and discover beneath Manchester. The opening of Liverpool's Williamson Tunnels and Stockport's Air Raid Shelters indicate public interest in underground spaces. Why not develop a range of these centres in and around Greater Manchester? There are groups campaigning for the re-opening of the Duke of Bridgewater's underground canals at Worsley and the Wet Earth colliery drainage tunnels at Clifton. There are promising possibilities within the City of Manchester.

Why not have boat trips along the Manchester and Salford Junction Canal tunnel, as happens in the Stanedge Tunnel on the Huddersfield Canal? The return journey could begin below the Great Northern Entertainment complex, up to Castlefield. There is enough space in the Victoria Arches to recreate an exhibition of the conditions during the Blitz, and a visitor centre devoted to subterranean Manchester. Further investigation of this site could exploit links with other tunnels. I understand that ideas have already been submitted to link the Arches with the Cathedral Visitor Centre.

The 'Guardian' telephone exchange would prove an exciting underground attraction. Inevitably the owners will point to the difficulties due to security, access, and health and safety reasons but while not underestimating the problems, it should not be beyond their capabilities and resources to open up at least a section of the complex. There have been occasional tours of the undercroft of Victoria Station, which has many features of interest - this could be further developed. Miners are campaigning for a memorial to those who lost their lives while working at the Bradford Colliery. There is surely space both for this, and also a visitor centre, for the colliery at the City of Manchester Stadium site.

Wooden pipe, and sewer reconstruction at the 'Underground Manchester' Exhibition

This book demonstrates that there is a body of information to interest and excite visitors. Tours and displays could be organised of tunnel systems built either for commercial purposes, or used as shelters during the last war, as well as the mysterious network of passages beneath the city. These sites and the emerging information demonstrate how the city could develop its already formidable tourism assets. It is time that the city recognized and benefited from the rich heritage concealed beneath its streets. This book has revealed at least some of Manchester's underground secrets - I am confident there is more to follow.

Publications

City Class and Culture (Ancoats Art Museum)
Ed by AJ Kidd & KW Roberts, Manchester University Press 1985

Just Henry. Memories of Bradford and Moston Collieries, Manchester
Henry Bairsto. Published by Neil Richardson 1991

The Lancashire & Yorkshire Railway vol 2,
John Marshall, David & Charles 1970

The Lost Rivers of Manchester
Geoffrey Ashworth. Willow Publishing 1987 (out of print)

GMAU Report, Manchester and Salford Junction Canal, November 1990

Manchester's Main Drainage System Past and Present
Geoffrey F Read, City Engineer & Surveyor 1979

Manchester Victoria Station
Tom Wray, Peter Taylor Publications 2004

A & G Murray and the Cotton Mills of Ancoats
I Miller, C Wild. Oxford Archaeology North 2007

The Piccadilly Triangle
UMAU June 2002

Salford in the Days of Steam
Paul Shackcloth, Steam Image 2004

War Plan UK: The Secret Truth about Britain's Civil Defence
Duncan Cambell, Paladin Books 1983 (out of print)

Websites

Manchester and Salford Junction Canal
www.subrit.org.uk

Guardian Telephone Exchange
www.cybertrn.demon.co.uk/guardian

CD

Manchester Underground - six broadcasts by Ken Howarth
North West Sound Archive, Clitheroe Castle, Clitheroe BB7 1AZ

Notes

Manchester and Salford Junction Canal

1   Manchester City News Notes & Queries [2948] [2963]
2   Air Raid Shelter Plans, Manchester Central Library Archives
3   Air Raid Precautions Special Committee minutes 1938-1939,
      Manchester Central Library Archives
4   The Manchester Village, Deansgate Remembered, Frank Heaton,
      Neil Richardson 1995
5   Manchester Evening News 9 March 2002
6   Letter from Mrs Neimec to Harry Smith
7   The Manchester Village, Deansgate Remembered, Frank Heaton,
      Neil Richardson 1995
8   Paper given by Ken Howarth 1978, in the author's private collection,
      and 'Manchester Underground' 1993, North West Sound Archive
9   Waterways Into Castlefield, John C Fletcher, Neil Richardson 1989

The Duke's Tunnel

1   UMAU Report June 2002, Piccadilly Triangle
2   Manchester City News Notes & Quotes 1879
3   Manchester City News Notes & Quotes 1883
4   Manchester City News Notes & Quotes 1879

Victoria Arches

1   Manchester Evening News 13 October 1960
2   Air Raid Precautions Special Commitee minutes 1938-1939,
      Manchester Central Library Archives
3   Manchester Cathedral Sound Archive
4   'Manchester Underground' 1993, North West Sound Archive

Guardian

1   Manchester Evening News 19 March 1983
2   Subterranea Britannica website & Stockport Express 19 October 2006

The City Centre

1   Dale Street Water Wheel Survey Report,
      Manchester Region Industrial Archaeology Society 1996
2   Manchester Guardian 18 February 1882
3   Manchester Evening Chronicle 19 May 1930
4   Manchester City News 30 March 1889 & Table of Pneumatic Tubes,
      The British Postal Museum and Archive
5   Manchester Guardian September 1874
6   A Well in Old Manchester, Prof Wright Baker,
      Lancashire & Cheshire Antiquarian Society 1959

Old Millgate and Market Place

1   The Archetypal Irish Cellar Dweller, Sandra Hayton,
      Manchester Region History Review 1998
2   Manchester Memories, George Mold 1972
3   Manchester Men & Manchester Streets, T Swindells 1908
4   Manchester City News 11 December 1903

Deansgate
1 'Manchester Underground' 1993, North West Sound Archive
2 Interview with the author 2007

Around Manchester and Parts of Salford
1 Interview with author 2007
2 Manchester Evening Chronicle 3 June 1936
3 Lancashire & Cheshire Antiquarian Society volume 1886
4 Manchester City News Notes and Queries [3,330] 1883
5 Manchester Rapid Transit Study November 1968
6 The Picc-Vic Project, Greater Manchester Passenger Transport April 1975

Rumours of tunnels and treasure
1 Stories and Tales of Old Manchester, selected by Cliff Hayes from Stories by Frank Hird

Final Thoughts
1 Slug's Reminscences

Acknowledgments

I want to begin with three underground Manchester pioneers who have had a major influence on the content and whose research, archives and photographs are the backbone of this book.

I would like to thank especially Joy Hancox, author of *The Byrom Collection*, *The Queen's Chameleon*, and *Kingdom For a Stage* for allowing me to consult her research and archives regarding underground Manchester. Following the discovery of a tunnel beneath her home in Higher Broughton she became interested in the history of the area and subsequently featured in a *Manchester Evening News* article and took part in two Granada Television programmes in the 1970s. (See section on Singleton Road). Many readers and viewers responded with letters of their own recollections of tunnels and underground passages, about which Joy made further enquiries. As a result she assembled a unique collection of material. Joy was already fully involved in the research and writing of other books and so she put this project to one side. Consequently her underground Manchester resource of letters, documents and interview notes built up over twenty years has remained untouched. I feel privileged that Joy has kindly given me first access to these files with the understanding that the correspondence she had received should be treated with respect and fairness, and the source acknowledged. This book contains a selection of those letters and I hope the writers or their descendants, will be pleased with the results.

The process of examining the collection was not only so extremely beneficial in my research but also a pleasurable experience because of Joy's excellent hospitality, patience, interest, and her generosity and support in also giving permission for various plans and photographs to be reproduced as well as her excellent update on William Connell.

Thanks also go to the late Harry Smith and his family for freely making his research notes, photographs and plans available to me. Harry, who died in 2006, has been described as the 'Fred Dibnah' of the tunnelling world. Nicknamed 'the human mole', he had spent the last fifty years pursuing his great passion of exploring and uncovering subterranean routes. Born in 1934, in Manchester, his first job was as an apprentice electrician at the coal face of Snipe Colliery in Ashton. On family holidays he became interested in the mines of mid Wales and the Peak District, then later in the old mines at Alderley Edge.

Harry's interest in underground Manchester began in the 1950s, following an invitation to dig out the Wishing Well Cafe shaft in Manchester. This was the beginning of many years researching, recording and uncovering tunnels around the City. Because of his tunnelling expertise, Harry ventured into many tunnels that others would not dare to enter. With the help of family and friends he assembled a valuable record of what lies below Manchester. His efforts sometimes brought him into conflict with the City Council, and was often frustrated by officialdom. In the late 1990s he wanted to continue working on the Duke of Bridgewater's canal tunnel at Castlefield which he believed ran further under the city, but the Council had other plans for the land and blocked any further work. Right up to his death, Harry was tireless in his efforts to establish the locations and record details of Manchester tunnels.

I am very appreciative of the help and advice given by Ken Howarth who has very kindly and generously given me use of his photo collection, and made available his paper on the Manchester and Salford Junction Canal, and of course for agreeing to write the Foreword for this book with its helpful introduction to the geology of the area.

I would like to acknowledge the help of: Tony France and Paul Sillitoe who have contributed important information. Warren Marshall, David Hilton and Colin Firth at Manchester City Council; Les Patterson for permission to use his photograph, and to his ex colleagues Bill Jones, Brian McNulty, Ken Ledson MBE from Manchester City Engineers Department; the staff of the Mitre Hotel; Ian Crossley and Eric Keasberry at United Utilities for their assistance in accessing the Manchester Sewer Archive; archivist Christopher Hunwick, and Verger Geoffrey Robinson at Manchester Cathedral; Bernard Champness of the Manchester Region Industrial Archaeology Society; John Hodgson at Rylands Library, Lionel Moore at H Marcel Guest Ltd, and David Lawless at the Manchester Royal Exchange.

Thanks also to Chris Hill for sharing his many contacts, and to Nick Catford for generously giving permission to use his photographs of the Manchester and Salford Junction Canal Tunnel.

I am also grateful to the many people whom I have contacted and without hesitation have shared what they know, including: John C Fletcher, Chris Makepeace, Keith Hamnet, Geoff Wellens, Jim Shutler, Don Lee, Gloria Gaffney, Alan Morrison, David McCarthy, Susan

Rogers, Bill Ashton, John Owen, Tom Caunce, Robert Holmes, Bill Newton, Margaret Geddes, Brian Maltby, Hazel Wilkinson-Wright, Barbara Frost, Steve Little, Bob Bonner and for the invaluable recollections of Norman Savory.

I am especially grateful to Alex Britton not only for his recollections and photographs of the Wishing Well restaurant but also for his help and suggestions of other information sources.

Special thanks to Dr Michael Powell at Chethams Library for all his assistance, and also to the staff of the Local Studies Libraries at Manchester and for permission to reproduce images from their collection. Also the staff at Salford, Tameside, Trafford, Stockport local studies libraries, Manchester County Records Office, Museum of Science and Industry Manchester, and Norman Redhead at the Greater Manchester Archaeology Unit.

I am indebted Terry Wyke for his good advice and for checking the manuscript.

My thanks to everyone who has helped me in my research, including anyone I may have inadvertently missed out, and I also express my appreciation of the many people who have told me about tunnels after my 'Manchester Down Below' talk.

Also to record my appreciation of Pat Gothard, Cynthia Hollingworth and to my wife Judy for their painstaking proof-reading and their suggested improvements to the wording.

Finally a thank you to my family and friends who have so graciously endured the endless chat about tunnels over the last few years.